17th June 1998.

Dee Hall

With true friedship,

Ford

Poor Little Rich Girl
(*Povera Ricca Bambina*)

Gemma Ford

Poor Little Rich Girl
(*Povera Ricca Bambina*)

By

Gemma Ford

New Millennium
292 Kennington Road. London SE11 4LD

British Library Cataloguing in Publication Data.
A catalogue record for this book is available
from the British Library.

Printed and bound by Morgan Technical Books Ltd.
Wotton-under-Edge, Gloucestershire.
Issued by New Millennium*
ISBN 1 85845 130 2
*An imprint of The Professional Authors' & Publishers' Association

Acknowledgements

My gratitude to Vicky and Ken for encouraging me to write
this book and to Beryl in Devon for her invaluable help
in getting it written."Thank you" also to sweet
Pamela and to my good friends, Beryl and
Eric and Vera and Eric, for their help
during the past year and to all
other good friends, from
Reggie and me.
Arrivederci!

For Reggie

My mother and father in 1920

CHAPTER I

Genova la Superba! It was May 1921. My father always wanted a girl, and here I was.

It was a lovely sunny day on the Riviera dei Fiori, which is situated on the coast near Genoa, and I was very happy to be born, at least, that was what they told me later. I was born with a smile on my face and I had a golden future waiting for me with great prospects for a worry free life. Unfortunately, things did not work out quite so well and my rosy existence lasted only until the beginning of the Second World War.

I was the second child of a relatively wealthy Italian family with aristocratic ties and land holdings in Italy and Somalia. I had one older brother, Filippo. My father's business was in cotton, grown on our African estates and processed in Genoa. I grew up without being spoilt, thanks to the strictness of a dutiful, but affectionate, governess. She would not stand any nonsense. My German grandmother, Margarethe, was also very strict, but she loved me very much and for that I will always be very grateful.

Soon after I was born, my father established new offices in Turin and Milan. His business was very successful at that time and he bought a large mansion in Turin. Our little family moved there when I was about two years old. We had several servants, including a butler from Somalia.

I spent my holiday's at my grandparent's villa in Varallo when I was a child. The villa was situated in a lovely part of the country in the Alps near the Swiss border and I got to know many of the local people in the area. I developed a friendship with another local girl, Carla. We were about the same age and we played together nearly every day. That friendship has endured to this day. Although Carla lives in Rome now, we still keep in touch.

Like other children, I was quite naughty from time to time. I remember once, as a little girl learning to play the piano, I hung two frogs in a pair of old gloves on to the candle holders of the piano and left them dancing on the keys. I was punished for that - no puddings for three days. Thank you Nonna!

At seven years of age, after private tuition in Italian and German at home, I began studying at a private school run by French nuns in Turin. I remember very little about my first school, except that I was not unhappy during the two years I was there, unlike the next school I attended.

My grandmother, Margarethe, died in 1930 and, although I was only nine years old, I remember my deep feelings of loss and sadness at her passing. In September of that year I was enrolled in a college in Genoa where the Mother Superior was my first cousin. Besides Italian, I still had lessons in German and French as well as ballet lessons. I also started to play tennis. Since then, ballet has been my favourite recreation and tennis my favourite sport.

However, I was very unhappy for most of my time at this college. I remember my first impressions of the place. It was austere and lonely. The dormitory was cold and sparsely furnished with iron beds. None of the other girls seemed to be very happy there either. Nevertheless, the college had a good reputation and it was expensive. The Mother Superior was distant and very authoritarian. I felt no sense of warmth or affection in her in spite of the fact that she was a relative. The only advantage I believe I gained from this school was to learn to be self-sufficient.

After my first unhappy year at college, I was surprised to be informed that I was to go to Rome, to have breakfast with the Pope! This was just after I had made my First Holy Communion when I was aged ten years. I travelled to Rome with my cousin, the Mother Superior, and I remember being enthralled to sit in my white communion dress at one end of a long table in one of the state rooms in the Vatican with Pio XI sitting at the opposite end. His holiness spoke paternally to me about my family and, in

2

particular, about my aunt Gemma, my father's sister, who became blessed after her death in 1926 and was proposed to be canonised as a saint. He expressed hopes that I too would lead such a saintly life. I assured His Holiness that I intended to follow in her footsteps. I meant it at that time because I was very excited at meeting the Pope and my dislike of nuns had not then fully matured.

On returning to the college, I continued my unhappy existence. I was feeling quite sorry for myself. Melodramatically or otherwise, I felt I was something of a *Povera Ricca Bambina*. Then, when I reached the age of thirteen years, my life began to change dramatically.

When my periods started, I panicked. I had not been warned about the changes that took place to a girl's body when puberty started and I thought something terrible was wrong with me. I confided in another, older, girl. She laughed and told me what was going on and also, gleefully it seemed, said it would continue for the rest of my life. This was a time when such subjects were never openly discussed in the family, or anywhere else for that matter. Unfortunately for me, the older girl told other girls and, soon enough, the nuns found out. Mother Superior was furious with me for not coming to her with my concerns. I could not tell her that I found her too cold and insensitive to approach and, in fact, the same could be said of the other nuns at the college.

Later that year, in December, I became ill. I felt dreadful. I was coughing and shivering for days and I really began to think I would die. I had severe chest pains and I knew I was suffering from something worse than a common cold. I saw a doctor only once. He was a gynaecologist. He prescribed a cough mixture! I wrote to my mother to tell her of my illness but, unknown to me, Mother Superior stopped my letter from being posted! I was confined to a room in the tower of the college. It had the usual iron bed with two blankets. I had only a nightdress to wear and I was freezing. There was a fierce wind outside rattling the window and the atmosphere of the room was so cold and eerie that I became very frightened. I felt that I was waiting to meet my maker. Apart from the one visit by the doctor, I saw no-one except the priest who came to give me holy communion every morning. The food consisted of a cup of milk and a piece of bread for breakfast with a bowl of soup for lunch and again for dinner. One morning I asked the priest if I was dying. He told me to pray for my soul to go to heaven!

Luckily for me, my mother, who had always been psychic, dreamed I was crying and calling for help. She woke my brother in the middle of the night. "Gemma is ill, you must go to see her. Telephone me as soon as you get there" He was sceptical about her claims that I was crying and in need of help but my mother insisted that he get in the car and drive to the college anyway, from Turin to Genoa! Filippo was about 22 years old then. When he arrived at the college, Mother Superior was very reluctant to let him see me. She told him everything was fine with me! She was probably embarrassed to let him see the conditions in the tower. My brother argued strongly to see me, however. Well, he could not return to mother to tell her he had failed to see me after she had insisted so forcefully. My dear cousin was obliged to show him to the room in the tower, my prison.

When the door of the room opened and I saw Filippo standing there, I burst into tears. He told me later that I looked ghastly. My hair was plaited but it had not been combed for many days. He approached my bed and embraced me. "Where is mama?" I sobbed at him. "She will be here today," he told me reassuringly. I was overcome with love for my brother and my family at that time. I suppose there was an element of self-pity attached to my emotions at the time, but I really was feeling very sick and my brother's was the only friendly face I had seen for some time.

My mother duly arrived later that morning. As soon as she saw me she telephoned one of the best lung specialists in Italy. He arrived later that day and immediately diagnosed pleurisy, in both lungs! He told my mother that if the condition was not treated immediately I could end up in a sanatorium for many years. I was too ill to be moved home to Turin and so it was arranged for me to be moved to a heated room on the second floor of the main building. I well remember being taken down the spiral stairway of the tower on a stretcher. I was put on a special diet and had to endure daily injections but I was never left alone again. My mother or my brother came every day to see that the necessary care was provided.

By the end of February 1935 I was pronounced well enough to move to convalescence. Turin was still too cold and it was decided to put me in an hotel in Rapallo, a resort on the Riviera near Genoa. My room had a balcony with a very nice view out over the sea. At another angle on the coast I could see a small castle. It was originally the prison for Rapallo but it was now in ruins. I asked my mother to bring my painting box from the college along with a small easel. I wanted to paint the castle.

That little painting gave me great pleasure for many years thereafter, even when I was facing terrible ordeals. Unfortunately, along with most of my other property and advantages, I lost it shortly after the war.

About one month later, I was back at the college. Although I hated the place, I was glad to see my class-mates again. In the summer, we had a special function in the college chapel. The final vows-taking of new nuns. The ceremony was conducted by His Eminence the Cardinal of Genoa in the presence of the nuns' families. The novices, wearing white bride's gowns and white veils, were spread-eagled on the floor during the ceremony. It was all very impressive. My dear cousin, the Mother Superior, hinted later that I would look ever so well when my turn came. I did not disillusion her right away, but I had no intention of becoming a nun. Thanks to the experiences I had of the college, all I wanted to do was to get away from nuns as quickly as I possibly could!

Shortly after my fifteenth birthday, my class got a new nun, sister Letizia. She was our Italian language teacher. She was more kindly towards me than the other nuns and I got on well with her. She frequently commended me for my essays and collected them to read out to the other pupils. I noticed her special interest in me and I was flattered by her attentions. She often came to see me in the dormitory with an affectionate smile on her face and she would give me her crucifix to kiss. After a while, she began kissing me affectionately on the forehead and I began to wonder why she did not do this to any of the other girls. Then, one night, she tried to kiss my lips! I froze. "Gemma," she whispered, "you are my precious stone." However, when she saw my horrified reaction and discomfort, she became abrupt, "you are a silly little girl," she fairly spat the words at me, and with that she turned and left with a flurry of her habit. My world was disintegrating! I was fifteen years old, but still very naive in terms of such worldly or peculiar matters. Today, such a tale would not even raise an eyebrow but to me then, it was unthinkable. I have never related this experience to anybody, until now. However, sister Letizia's gender confusion did not remain a secret for very long. Somebody else must have had similar contact with her because, very quickly after my experience, she disappeared to a convent leaving behind some whispering and giggling among the girls.

I was obliged to stay at the college for another year. I was firmly resolved not to become a nun. My experiences of them were not good, shocking in at least that one case, and, although I kept my faith and have kept it to this day, by then I had come to realise that God and religious beliefs were not the sole prerogative of the clergy.

A family photograph taken when I was about 10 months old.

In the garden of our house in Turin with the family butler.

Nine years old. At a children's party just before I went to college.

Grandfather, Giovanni, and grandmother, Margarethe. Circa 1910.

CHAPTER II

My father, Tito, stayed well out of politics. He was a wise and prudent man. He never discussed politics, at least not outside the family. From remarks he made to my mother from time to time, I gathered that he foresaw the trouble that was looming over the European scene at an early stage. Because his business in cotton meant he had many dealings with British companies and businessmen, he was pro-British and he was worried about the possibility of war. My mother was also very friendly with many of their English acquaintances. Most of the furniture in our home, even the Big Ben grandfather clock, was of English origin and she bought Filippo's clothing in London whenever they visited England. My mother and father both spoke fluent English.

I too had no interest in politics at that time, or since then for that matter. My later experiences with the German Wehrmacht was strictly non-political. As a teenager, I was more concerned with my own predicament and, by 1937, I was facing an important decision about my life. My father's family wanted me to become a nun! However, I had no vocation for that sort of life. I was not sure how my family would react to my refusal. But I was determined to avoid being forced to adopt a life that I did not feel appropriate for myself. In those days, acting against the wishes of your parents was a serious step. It was possible to become an outcast from the family as a result. Nevertheless, I was adamant and stubbornly resisted all efforts to induce me to change my mind.

One day during the summer holidays, I was summoned urgently by another cousin. He was much older than me and he was the headmaster of another college near Turin. That day he was waiting for me in the college chapel and he came straight to the point as soon as I arrived. "Gemma," he said bluntly," your father tells me you refuse to go back to college as a novice in

September. Is that true?"

I confirmed my position and, at the very moment I spoke, I visualised myself dressed as a novice dancing a pirouette in front of a flabbergasted Mother Superior. I had been thinking about the ballet on my way to the meeting and, now, the imaginary scene amused me but my cousin must have seen a smile on my face because he went on, with some relish I felt, "In that case, I am instructed to tell you it has been arranged for you to go away as an *au-pair*. You will be with a very respectable, nice, family. The lady is a widow and she has to take over her husband's business She needs a reliable person to look after her four children. They live at Saint Alessio in a villa in the hills near Alba. The lady will take you there next Sunday." That was the way he delivered the news and, with a satisfied smile on his face, he left me standing gaping with surprise.

It was a decision of my father's family. I was only sixteen and that was my punishment. However, I was not too upset because it also meant that I was not to be condemned to a life of hypocrisy as a nun. Although I hated the college and disliked most of its staff, I loved the learning I achieved there. I was doing quite well, especially in Italian and other languages as well as history and geography. I had tears in my eyes and I felt numb with sadness at the thought of leaving all my school friends.

So that was the way they took the decision over my life. When I think about it now it seems as though we were still living in the mediaeval era. The independence enjoyed by today's generation of young people is staggering by comparison. I left the college for good shortly after that. I revisited the place only once, many years later. By then, it had closed down as a school and part of it was operating as a kindergarten. I had no feeling of nostalgia or regret at its closure. As a school, I believe it made most of its pupils unhappy during their stay. There is no evidence that high academic standards are derived only through the medium of strict discipline and Spartan conditions.

It was in August 1937 that I started my first job. The lady of the house was a very nice woman. She was running her late husband's business and she had a lot of different responsibilities but she always was very considerate and very understanding. She did not approve of my departure from school at such a young age but when I explained to her the reasons, she was most supportive. Her youngest child, Carlo, was twelve years old. Luckily the children were quite well behaved and I had no great difficulty in keeping them occupied with games and recreation under control. However, one day when we went on an outing. Carlo, running down a slope near a railway line, was nearly run down by an oncoming train. I just had time to grab him by the sleeve to pull him clear. I will never forget his frightened look or my own trembling reaction to the shock of the incident.

I left Saint Alessio in 1939. The lady had sold the business and gone with her children to live in America. I was eighteen years old by then and, for the first time, I was going to visit Germany. I was going with my mother to Freiburg, near the French border, to visit friends of the family. I was longing to spend more time with my mother because, during the previous few years, I had not seen much of my parents. My mother was always very busy with her social life and my father was travelling around the world because of his business in cotton plantations in Somalia.

My family connections with Germany were on my mother's side. My maternal grandfather, Giovanni, was an Italian artist who had worked in Germany. He had a studio in Munich and practised as an architect and architectural sculptor. It was there that he met and married my German grandmother, Margarethe. They had three children, my mother, Elsa, and two sons. My grandfather had gained a fine reputation for his works of art in Munich and for his works on King Ludwig II's castles, Linderhof and Herrenchiemsee, in Bavaria. When he retired, his grandson, Carl, took over the studio. Carl won German government contracts and, because of his Italian

13

connections and artistic inclinations, he recruited over 300 Italian workers for the building of the new Chancery in Berlin. During our stay in Freiburg we received an invitation from Carl to visit his family in Berlin.

The journey from Freiburg to Berlin was very pleasant. We went by train on the Mitropa, the German National Railway, through the beautiful scenic country from the South to the North, passing near the secret Siegfried Line! The sense of impending war was already in the air. We arrived at dawn at the Anhalter Railway Station to be welcomed by my mother's nephew, Carl, and driven to the Hotel Adlon in the Kurfurstdendam in the centre of the city. There we were met by Max, Carl's son. Over the course of the next few days he showed us around Berlin and he left us with wonderful memories.

Max was an officer in the German Army. He was brilliant. He was very handsome, showing a strong trace of the Italian blood that determined his features. I was very attracted to him. The feeling was mutual and we spent a few happy days together. We agreed to meet again in the near future, but the war intervened and I never saw him again. He was just twenty-five years old when he was killed on the Eastern Front a couple of years later. I was broken-hearted when I heard that tragic news.

Three days before we left Berlin, Carl rang us: "I have a surprise for you," he said to my mother. "An audience with the Führer at the chancery in the Wilhemstrasse!" He had met Hitler several times already and he had mentioned our visit to Freiburg to the German leader. Hitler had invited him to bring us to the chancery.

It was just after the opening of the new chancery and we would be able to see the Italian artistic work done on the building. I confess to a feeling of excitement at the prospect of meeting such an important political leader. Hitler and his new Third Reich was being discussed every day in newspapers and on radio. By all accounts, he was the most important figure in European politics at that time. The German people expected great things of him.

On the morning of the visit, a large Mercedes limousine arrived at our hotel to collect us. The chauffeur treated us like royalty. It made me feel very important. My mother was nervous but I began to relish the pomp and circumstance of the occasion. When we arrived at the chancery, the chauffeur opened the car doors and we were met by a uniformed officer wearing epaulettes. He conducted us through the main entrance and into a large state room. Everybody present seemed to be in uniform except myself, mother and uncle Carl. Max was not present, to my regret.

Shortly after our arrival, another officer came and conducted us around some of the larger rooms of the building. I remember at one point uncle Carl was speaking about several features of the designs with another distinguished looking man who he later identified to my mother as Albert Speer, the chief architect for the building of the chancery and one of Hitler's favourites. Although we were supposed to admire the artistic elements of the architecture, I remember very little of anything I saw. I think the domination of the uniforms combined with the typical Germanic heel clicking and other formalities, were too overpowering to enable me to absorb much of the details of walls, pillars or art-works. There seemed to be a sense of 'the quiet before the storm' about the place.

When that tour concluded, we were shown into another large, long, room. At the far end stood Adolf Hitler! He was standing under a huge black eagle mounted on the wall behind him and with an enormous writing desk in front. For an instant I had the impression he was a wax model. His pose was statuesque, his left arm held Napoleon style with his fingers slipped into the tunic of his military uniform.

We approached in a small group with the equerry. I had expected to shake hands but, instead, he gave us a Nazi salute! He seemed to stare at us. His eyes were extraordinarily blue and penetratingly intense. I began to feel bit uneasy. He said a few words of welcome and thanked uncle Carl for a good job. He then asked my mother a few questions about our trip and our home region. He appeared to be impressed by the fluency with which we spoke German. He asked me if I had any plans to emulate my grandfather and become an artist. I answered, rather awkwardly, that I was interested in painting. He replied that painting was a passion of his own life but that he now found little time to pursue his pastime. I wanted to elaborate and tell him about my pictures of Rapallo Castle, but I was too uneasy in his presence and I could not relax sufficiently to make conversation. I simply dried up. At that point, he smiled at me. It was a distant sort of smile and I had the impression throughout this brief meeting that his thoughts were elsewhere. Then, he turned to uncle Carl and thanked him again for his contribution to the building of the chancery. He paid a compliment to our family for its artistic endeavours over the years and, with that, the audience ended and the equerry led us out of the room.

That was just a few weeks before Germany invaded Poland and started the Second World War. I believe the plans for the invasion had already been put into effect and that was why the heavy sense of imminent war was in the air. Many of the people at the chancery must have known what was planned and, although nothing was said openly, it accounted for the general atmosphere at the time.

We were escorted back to the car and driven to back to the hotel. I had hoped to see Max again before we left Berlin but he had been recalled to his unit and we were not able to meet.

The war was near and my life was due to change enormously, but I did not realise that just then. What I did realise was that the visit to the chancery and the meeting with Hitler had left me feeling nervous for the future. Before the visit, I had, naturally I believe, been excited at the prospect of meeting the man who was said to be the founding father of a new 'thousand year reich'. Afterwards,

I felt only a sense of foreboding. Yet, my meeting with the Führer was to stand me in good stead later when I had to deal with the Wehrmacht and SS officers who occupied Italy.

We left Berlin the following day and returned to Freiburg to finish our vacation. However, a few days after that, orders came for all foreigners with passports to leave Germany. My mother and I were, of course, Italian passport holders. We left Germany and went by train back to Italy a couple of weeks before the war started. At that time my parents had separated but my mother and I were still living in the family villa in Turin.

My grandfather, Giovanni, in his studio in Munich. Circa 1890.

Uncle Giuseppe in his studio in Mogadishu. Circa 1922.

CHAPTER III

The war started with the German invasion of Poland on September 1st 1939. At first, Italy was not involved in the war and our lives at home continued normally enough, although the effects of the war were felt in Italy as well. Then, in June of 1940, Italy joined Germany in a war against Britain and France. Before long, Turin was being bombed. It seemed that we were forced to live for much of the time, day and night, in an air-raid shelter.

Finally, we decided to get away from the constant threat of bombing in Turin and leave for the family villa which was situated just outside a picturesque little town called Varallo in the Alpine region of Valsesia, near the Swiss Border. It was my maternal grandparent's home, built for the summer holidays by my grandfather in the town where he was born. Every year they left Munich to spend the summer months at the villa and they lived there permanently after my grandfather retired. He died in 1927 and my grandmother, Margarethe, continued to live there until she died in 1930. Another uncle, Eugenio, who was a painter, had lived alone there since that time.

It was lovely building, like a small castle, on a hillside surrounded by dense forest at the back and in the front by a large garden with many beautiful sculptures. They were all made by my other uncle, Giuseppe, who was also a sculptor and artist. He had died in Somalia some years earlier.

As a little girl I had spent my summer holidays there with my grandmother and those were the best and happiest times of my youth. Now, here I was again, very happy to have escaped from the horror of the bombed city to the peace and tranquillity of the countryside. There were quite a few small villages around this one little town and I was able to re-acquaint myself with many of the local people of the region who I had known as a child.

But that peace and tranquillity was not to last! One lovely morning in September 1942 as I was walking towards the main street of the town, I was approached by two German soldiers on a motorcycle and sidecar. They stopped asked me, in poor Italian, for the location of the town hall. They were very surprised when I answered in fairly faultless German. They thanked me for the directions and drove off with a roar of their motorcycle engine. I went straight back home to tell my mother. "The Germans are here!" She gave me a frightened look. On reflection, it was a grave mistake for me to have revealed my fluency in German to these soldiers because it was to lead to my recruitment by the German army and, ultimately, to my own ruin.

One morning, about a week later, a large black staff-car with German military flags on its wings, stopped at the gate of the villa. Two officers in German uniform rang the bell. My uncle sent the gardener to open the gate and the two officers came up the flight of steps. At that moment my mother called to me "Mouse, (her pet name for me), go upstairs." She was worried, not knowing what was happening.

She and uncle met them at the main entrance and then led them to the reception room. After introducing themselves, they asked my mother if she had a daughter. Probably sensing her alarm, they went on quickly to tell her that they had been informed by some soldiers that they had met some young woman who spoke good German. They had established my identity and the location of our villa from the mayor at the town hall. They needed an interpreter very urgently for the opening of the German *Kommandatur* in the next two days. My mother stalled them for a minute, saying that she thought she could help, and offered them tea. They accepted and she then had an opportunity to talk to my uncle. She wanted to volunteer herself in my place but after some heated discussion, they both agreed that the request was a relatively harmless offer of temporary employment. After all, our country was allied with Germany and my uncle was worried about the possibility of a reprisal if the German officers believed our family was hostile by refusing what appeared to be a reasonable request to meet me. The villa, with its many valuable collections, was very precious to him. My mother was, probably, more concerned about my virtue at the idea of my associating with handsome, protestant, German officers.

In the event, my mother came upstairs and escorted me down to meet the two officers. I was introduced to the more senior of them first, a captain, Hauptmann Sigurd Wagner. He was an Austrian, from Vienna. The other officer was Oberleutnant Heinz Leigh from Hanover. After the handshakes and introductory conversation, I immediately became *Fraulein Emmy*. I have to say that both officers behaved like perfect gentlemen. Furthermore, in all my later experiences with regular German officers, I was never once treated discourteously. In fact, I became very popular with my new employers and I was able to influence a few decisions they made from time to time. One of those little influences I managed to exercise was to save my life later.

The Germans had rented a villa in the town as a location for their *Kommandatur*. Captain Wagner was responsible for the whole region of Valsesia. Within a week of my starting my new job, news spread around the little town that the local *Signorina* was the new interpreter at the *Kommandatur*. My job was mainly concerned with translating documents from German to Italian and vice versa. I also helped to dispense ration cards and it was not very long before a seemingly endless queue built up at the back entrance of the building. People were coming to the *Kommandatur* seeking ration cards for brown bread and powdered milk. They were mostly elderly people or young mothers with children. They were difficult times for everybody and food was only available with ration cards. The German army supplies for the *Kommandatur* arrived only every three weeks from Milan. It was very difficult to

21

Our villa in Varallo

One of the sculptures at the villa.

keep everybody happy, but we were successful most of the time.

One sad episode occurred one night. The warehouse where all the rationed food for the civilian population was stored, was broken into and all the food was looted. This caused a good deal of suffering for the local people who depended on the supplies dispensed from the warehouse. To replace the rations I had to ask the HQ in Milan to send a fresh supply with the next transport. Luckily it was due in a few days and we were all very fortunate that the German *Kommandatur* was not under the control of the SS!

I remember one evening we were all invited to the captain's office to listen to the BBC's German language broadcast of the news! These soldiers of the *Kommandatur* were part of the regular Wehrmacht, normal family men doing their duty in wartime and hoping the war would finish soon. As time went by I became very friendly with the Captain Wagner. He had pledged to my mother that no harm would come to me and he saw to it that none of the troops under his command made any advances towards me. He was a kind, fatherly, family man himself and his moral standards were very high.

As the war progressed, news from the various axis fronts, especially North Africa and Russia, became less enthusiastic. Uncle Carl wrote to my mother to tell her the sad news of the death of his son Max. When I was told that Max had been killed, I was devastated. I cried a lot about that. The Captain Wagner and the other Germans were very sympathetic. But, by this time almost all of them were regularly receiving news of the death of relatives of their own and people they knew. In spite of the fact that German and Italian government propaganda was telling us things were going very well, the truth was being relayed by other media, especially by the BBC, and by wounded soldiers and those returning for leave. Things generally started to change for the worse.

During this period, the partisans were becoming more active

in our region and those who were caught were either shot on the spot or shipped off to Germany. The notorious SS had moved into the region and occasionally visited our town. Whenever they visited the *Kommandatur* I stayed out of sight. I did not like the looks of these SS men. They were arrogant and they treated the local people with contempt. They all seemed to have an intense look about them that reminded me of the look in the eyes of their leader when I had met him in Berlin.

Our office also received a lot of anonymous letters from around the region making accusations against other Italian citizens. Mostly they were concerned with ration offences but, occasionally, there were some accusing individual people or families of partisan involvement. The SS were responsible for counter-partisan operations, supposedly in collaboration with Italian forces, and I knew how dangerous these denunciatory letters could be, true or false, if the SS received them. I destroyed any that came my way, provided they were unsigned, as I knew there was no evidence of their arrival.

Our own good captain, on the other hand, was more dismissive of these unsigned letters but, rather than risk destroying them without authority, I decided to approach him on the subject to get permission to dispose of them all. I took a couple of examples of the less serious letters, those making allegations about people misusing ration cards. I waited for a less busy period and then went to his office. I asked the Captain what I should do with all the anonymous letters arriving at my office which contained all sorts of accusations. I showed him the examples and told him these were occupying a lot of our time. I remember saying to him; "If we have to investigate all of these letters we will not have time to do anything else." I then said that in my opinion we should just ignore them because they were mostly just vexatious and motivated out of envy or commercial rivalry. "Yes Fraulein Emmy" he said with a smile, "Just throw them in the dustbin!" I was glad to carry out his order and I destroyed any such letters that arrived at the *Kommandatur* from then on, anonymous or otherwise.

The months passed until Christmas 1943 came and everybody was busy sending parcels to their loved ones at home. I went to town with the Captain Wagner to help him to select a small bicycle for his little boy who was just five years old. In order to despatch it to Vienna by army post he had to take the bicycle to pieces and send it in three different parcels. After Christmas, a lovely photograph arrived from the captain's wife showing his little boy sitting on the reassembled bicycle!

During the first few months of 1943 news and rumours about North Africa and the Eastern Front were becoming increasingly pessimistic for the Axis. At the same time, the partisans were increasing their attacks against German and fascist targets in the region. Consequently, the struggle against the partisans was intensified with more and more involvement by the SS and regular German army. Many hundreds of young men were arrested, but most of them were being held on suspicion and did not really belong to the *Brigate Garibaldine*, as the partisan units were known. I had known quite a few of these men and their families when we were all children during the times I stayed with my grandparents at the villa. I had the feeling I should do something to help them.

One morning I took courage and went to the captain's office. *"Herr Hauptman"* I started, "I would like to put a proposal to avoid the arrest of so many men who don't belong to the partisan units. These suspects are being detained needlessly and it is clogging up the prisons and occupying much time to process and investigate each one thoroughly. Many of them are being arrested, held for a few weeks and then released anyway. Then many of them are re-arrested and the process is repeated. The SS are arresting people in the area simply because they are younger men and they do not know them or are not aware that they have recently been cleared of involvement with the *Brigate Garibaldine*. I happen to know

26

some of them well and I can vouch for them. If it is possible to give them some sort of identity card issued from the *Kommandatur*, with the office seal and their name and address on it, we could make them appear here every couple of weeks for renewal so that they can be monitored. This would avoid overloading the prisons and save time for the investigators to let them pursue the real *Brigate Garibaldine*. It will also save innocent and harmless people from being deported, or even executed, because they cannot be cleared in time."

Captain Wagner listened carefully and then gave me an amused look. I believe to this day that he knew I was, at least, not sympathetic to the fascists and I believe he secretly shared that lack of sympathy. Nevertheless, he was a loyal German officer. "I would have to clear this with the SS commandant, " he replied after some thought. "But what you say is true and we are spending too much time on these cases of mere suspects. There is a lot of injustice involved, as you say." I was on tenter-hooks for a moment while he considered the idea. "And who will do all the work involved in issuing these identity cards, *Fraulein Emmy?*"

I answered immediately, "Me, *Herr Hauptman.*"

He considered for another few moments "Right," he said, "draft a letter to the SS commandant for me, explain why this proposal should be put into effect. If they approve it you can start preparing the documentation."

I almost skipped out of his office! I was so relieved, because I knew I could help my own people. The same day I typed the letter and sent it up to the captain for his signature.

Two days later, the regional SS commandant and another SS officer arrived at the *Kommandatur* in an armoured staff car. They were with the captain for about fifteen minutes. Then they came down together and the captain introduced me to the steely, blue-eyed, blond commandant. "*Fraulein Emmy*," he said to me clicking his heels, "I understand you have German blood, and you actually met our Führer." The other officer said nothing but his gaze was not friendly. The captain knew about my uncle Carl and my trip to Berlin before the war began and, obviously, he had mentioned this to the SS officers. I confirmed my meeting with Hitler, in a tone of great respect, displaying as much pride as I could muster for the 'privilege' of meeting the Führer. I related the details very briefly in as friendly a way as I could, in spite of my nervousness. I was more nervous meeting these particular SS officers than when I had met their Führer in Berlin! I was not sure if Captain Wagner had told them the proposal to issue identity cards was my idea. I was frightened they might suspect I was trying to help partisans. The SS were known Nazi fanatics and even regular Wehrmacht officers seemed uneasy when they were around. They looked down on Italian people and they had a reputation for cruelty. However, I assume my German blood, albeit only one quarter, meant something to them and my meeting with Hitler obviously impressed them because, when I finished my story about our trip to the chancery, the commandant congratulated me for my family's services to the reich. He gave me a thin smile, shook my hand and clicked his heels again before turning to leave. My heart was pounding as they walked away with the captain.

Subsequently, the SS agreed to the new procedure and, the very next day, I was busy starting my new task of preparing the ID cards. Over the course of the next few days I had to collate all the names and addresses of the suspects in a list and then meet the printer who was to produce the identity cards. He was a family friend and the owner of the local newspaper. He also used to publish, from time to time, some of my little poems and short stories. As I was very busy by day dealing with the public and doing translations, I had to stay in the office late to get this extra work done, but it was all worthwhile and the identity cards were ready in a few days.

After that, we began to issue the cards to lots of, mostly

In my office at the *Kommandatur.* 1943.

The villa used as the *Kommandatur* in Varallo.

young, men. They were delighted to receive them. Some of them were released from prison as soon as they got a card and, no doubt, some were able to continue to support the partisans in the same way they had done before their arrest. To some extent the cards served to give clearance to real partisan activists. However, most of those issued with the cards were innocent of any involvement and I like to think I helped to stop some deportation or executions.

The remainder of 1943 saw one reverse after another for the Axis. The Allies invaded Sicily in July. Mussolini was overthrown within two weeks of the Allied landings on Italian soil. Two months later the Allies landed on the Italian mainland. The new Italian government surrendered but the Germans immediately occupied the whole Northern part of the country, including Rome. In the South, as far as Naples, the Allies were in control. There was much confusion in the country. The partisans were beginning to clear the German and Italian fascist forces out of many regions in the North. They were constantly attacking German garrisons and the reprisals were becoming more and more savage.

By the beginning of 1944 there was a general air of uncertainty among the remaining German troops in Italy. Nobody, except the diehard Nazis, was talking about victory at that time. The news from all fronts was hopeless. My mother and uncle were also becoming deeply concerned about possible partisan attacks against our family because I worked at the *Kommandatur*. We discussed the possibilities of my leaving to hide in the hills but, as the partisans controlled most of the country, outside the towns and main roads, it seemed I had nowhere to run. It would have been impossible to escape. Because I was employed by the Germans, any effort to leave would have been regarded as desertion, with serious consequences if I was caught by either side. I was feeling like a *Povera Ricca Bambina* again!

In June of 1944 the Allies launched their D- Day offensive

31

into France and, the same month, they entered Rome. That was a signal for the Germans to prepare for a general withdrawal from Italy. Gradually, the Allies were pushing North and the Germans seemed to be on the verge of collapse. The news from the Eastern Front was appalling with the Soviets entering Poland and threatening Austria from Hungary and the Balkans.

We continued working at the *Kommandatur* for another few months but, by then, only token efforts were made to carry on business as usual. The captain told me privately one day that he thought the Wehrmacht would make a last stand at the Brenner pass to protect Austria and Germany from the Allies advances. He told me not to worry about my own safety as he would make arrangements for my family to be moved to a safe area.

CHAPTER IV

The end was near! At the beginning of February 1945 new orders came through! The *Kommandatur* was to be transferred to another town, Alessandria, near Turin. I thought my job would finish once the Germans left our town. However, when I asked Captain Wagner, he told me that I was to move with them and continue my work for the present. He also reassured me that myself and my mother would not be left behind to the mercy of the partisans.

Soon afterwards, on a cold, grey, morning our column of about twenty vehicles left Varallo and headed towards the new destination. We were attacked and bombed by Allied aircraft three times on the way to Alessandria. These scenes were chaotic. Our column was forced to disperse off the road while the aircraft were around and myself and mother were terrified, as much by the machine guns firing back at the attacking aircraft as by the aircraft themselves. The first two attacks did no damage but the last attack was devastating. Two of the trucks was completely destroyed by bombs. Several soldiers were killed and others wounded. It took more than an hour to clear the road and deal with the dead and wounded. That was the first time I had seen any real fighting. It was a shocking experience for myself and mother, but we pressed on.

As soon as we arrived we took possession of the new HQ building. It was a huge building with a high glass tower. There were quite a few holes in the tower and scars on the walls of the main building from earlier bombing and strafing. There was no lift and we had to walk up and down many flights of stairs in the course of the day's work.

Two months passed and everybody was aware that the end of the war was near. Mussolini and his mistress, Clara Petacci, were captured and shot by partisans at Giulino di Mezzegra, near the Swiss border, in April. I was truly sorry to hear about Clara Petacci. Everybody knew she had no involvement in politics but she stayed with Mussolini to the very end and lost her life out of love and loyalty. A couple of days later, we heard that Hitler and his wife, Eva Braun, were also dead. My mother was very concerned. It was now obvious that the Germans would surrender soon. By this time, we began to realise that our lives were in danger because the partisans were known to be shooting people indiscriminately for 'collaboration'.

One day, without saying a word to me, my mother went to see the bishop at his residence to seek asylum for us. She rang the bell and the bishop came to the door. In those days there was not much etiquette left. My mother asked if he would help by giving us refuge in his residence for just a few days. The bishop knew me well, because, on previous occasions when he had experienced difficulty in getting rations or travel permits, I had helped him in various ways. However, that day all such past favours were forgotten! Without a word, he just slammed the door in my mother's face. Christian charity was dead! My mother came to my office very distressed later that day to tell me what had happened.

By coincidence the good captain Wagner was there at the moment my mother entered. He listened and then he reassured my mother that he had already provided a horse and carriage with an old coachman to enable us to reach my cousin's estate in Novi Ligure, which was situated about twenty kilometres from Alessandria.

The German army's surrender to the Allies in Italy took place at this time but the good captain did not want to surrender to the partisans, who would probably not have taken any prisoners, and so they were holding out until Allied army units arrived. In the early morning hours of May 4th my mother and I left in the horse-drawn coach. As we passed the army barracks, Captain Wagner, the lieutenant, and most of the other German military personnel were

34

standing in a silent salute to wish us goodbye.

I had tears in my eyes at that sad sight. Later, I found out that the good captain never saw his wife and child again. He was taken prisoner but, when he was released, he returned to Vienna to find out that his wife had killed their son and committed suicide rather than wait for the Russians to enter the city.

Halfway to Novi Ligure I had a premonition of disaster. I shouted for the coachman to stop between some high banks on the roadside. I was just in time! At that very instant, an aircraft appeared from nowhere, diving steeply with its machine-guns firing on to the road ahead of us. It was a miracle nobody was hurt. Luckily, it made only one pass and it rose again and roared away into the sky having done no damage.

We were then travelling through an area that was in the hands of the partisans. Suddenly, two men in irregular partisan dress appeared from the side of the road and stopped the carriage. One of them had a machine-gun and the other had a pair of pistols stuck in his waistband. They were also carrying two heavy bags. They asked us for a lift. We were in no position to refuse and they jumped into the carriage laughing cheerfully. "We just killed twenty fascists" one said. He opened one of the bags and I saw it was full of bloodstained clothes and loot. My mother, pale and distressed, never said a word and we were both very relieved when they left the coach a few kilometres further on, perhaps for another wild action.

We arrived at my cousin's estate to find that everybody had evacuated the place some weeks earlier. Only a handful of the farmers were still there to keep the estate going. One of the farmers provided us with accommodation in his farmhouse. There was a lot of talk among the locals about the partisans making reprisals against collaborators and my mother was becoming more and more worried about my fate. Naturally, we did not tell anybody that I had worked for the Germans. Shortly after our arrival in Novi Ligure

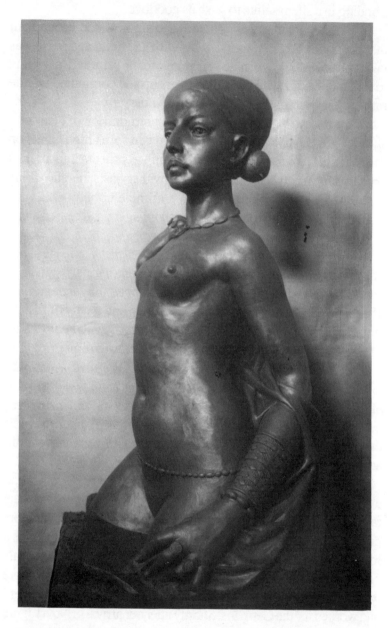

Sculpture from Mogadishu, now in the Colonial Museum, Rome.

Another sculpture from Mogadishu. Colonial Museum, Rome.

the war ended with the surrender of Germany.

Sooner or later we had to decide when to go back to Turin. My mother did not want to return to our home too soon because she was afraid of what might happen to me. I told her I had nothing to worry about. I had a clear conscience as I had only worked for the Germans as a civilian interpreter and I assumed, naively as it turned out, that it was not really a serious matter. Besides, I had not exactly volunteered for the job! A new Italian government structure with Prince Umberto at its head had been established under Allied control and we began to feel the days of partisan excesses were over. I persuaded my mother that it would be best to go back home as soon as possible. On the morning we left the estate, the farmer's wife gave me a present, a lovely little goose in a basket. We soon became friends. I named her 'Rosetta'!

The journey back to Turin was a nightmare. We had to walk four miles to the nearest railway station and change trains three times. 'Rosetta' in the basket stayed silent until the conductor came to ask for our tickets. Then, she started shrieking, so I had to pay for her as well. I didn't mind, she was so lovely.

At last we arrived back home in the beginning of June. It was a nice warm summer but our family had to face a bleak future. The war and its aftermath left my father's business in ruins. The cotton plantations in Somalia were lost. The family home in Turin was put up for sale and all three of the company's offices, in Turin, Genoa and Milan, were closed down.

The only things that had been salvaged from the estates in Somalia were the sculptures of my uncle Giuseppe, who had made those lovely statues in the gardens of the villa in Varallo. After he died in Mogadishu, the Duke of Abruzzi, a cousin of the King of Italy, provided for the shipment of all ten sculptures to Italy where they were donated by my grandfather to the Italian Government. They can still be seen at the Colonial Museum, Valle Giulia, in Rome.

38

My mother and I were now living in a small rented flat on the outskirts of Turin. Life was a struggle. Everything was in short supply and we had to go without things that, in earlier years, we had in abundance.

At 5am on one very hot morning at the beginning of July, I was woken by a loud knocking on our door. It was the carabinieri. They had come to arrest me! My mother was shocked and crying and, I confess, I was quite frightened. The carabinieri, however, were very kind and understanding. They gave me plenty of time to get ready and to say goodbye to my mother, and to little 'Rosetta'. I said to myself "you must be brave. You have no reason to reproach yourself and you have done nothing to be ashamed of," and so, *a testa alta* (with head up), I went to prison!

I was not expecting very much, but what I found was sheer hell. I had painted the outside of a prison once, that at Rapallo, but I had never seen the inside of one before. The place was appalling. The beds in the cells were just sacks full of smelly, damp straw. In the women's section there were six of us in a cell of less than four metres square. There were no proper beds, no running water, and no lavatory. The latrine bucket was emptied by one of the inmates every morning. I had to take my turn for that particularly unpleasant chore.

The place was alive with cockroaches. We used to bet on the number each of us could kill in the course of the night. Our daily food was put through a shutter in the door. Breakfast consisted of a mug of brown water and a piece of brown bread. The main meal, if it can be called that, consisted of a plate of thin soup and another piece of brown bread. Friends and relatives were allowed to bring extra food for prisoners but the visits were confined to once a week only. I was very pleased to see my mother on these weekly visits as she was able to bring me some food in spite of her own shortages.

After three weeks in that dungeon, the order came for me to

be transferred back to Varallo, the scene of 'my crimes' during the war. Two uniformed carabinieri escorted me there on the train. They seemed to think my case was relatively minor and I began to feel less worried for myself. Halfway, we stopped at the station of Novara to change trains. The carabinieri bought me a drink and left me with two briefcases. "We know you will not run away," they said, smiling. They came back after one hour and at midnight we arrived at our destination. The two carabinieri said goodbye and then handed me over to the custody of the partisans waiting outside the station. These men were much less friendly and pushed me along the road. I was taken to the small prison in the town.

So, I was back in Varallo. In the moonlight, through the cell window I could see the villa on the top of the hill. I had tears in my eyes as I looked again at the home of my happy childhood. I was the only prisoner but, at least, conditions in this little provincial lockup were better than the hell-hole I had left in Turin. Soon the news of my arrest went around the town like wild fire. In the early morning a small crowd was standing at the entrance, asking why I was arrested. I was relieved to know that the local people did not regard me as an enemy or a collaborator. After two days my uncle got permission to visit me. He had remained at my grandparent's villa. It was a tearful reunion. He reassured me that the whole town was on my side and that I would be released in due course without any serious penalties. How wrong he was!

The next day, I underwent a cross-examination. I was taken to a large room in the prison. I noticed that all the partisans present were from another valley. Not one of them belonged to the local brigade. At the first hearing they wanted to know what was my job in the *Kommandatur* and the names of Italian people who had helped the Germans and acted as informers. My answers were categorical. "I have never been a spy or an informer before and I don't want to become one now! My job was as an interpreter dealing with relations between the *Kommandatur* and the local people." I protested that I did not have such information anyway. They were very aggressive in their attitudes and the chief interrogator threatened me with a firing squad if I did not give him the names of people who had betrayed partisans to the Germans.

After what seemed like several hours of repetitious questions and answers they took me back to my cell. My mother was waiting for me. She had travelled from Turin that morning. Somebody had told her that it was the last time she would see her daughter alive! It was heartbreaking trying to console her and to reassure her that my predicament was not all that bad, although, I was, by then, very worried myself.

The next day I had a visit from a priest. He was chaplain to the partisans. He offered me a confession and absolution for my terrible crimes! I declined because I did not feel in any way sinful at that time. However, I began to get even more worried that I was really going to be shot without any proper trial. The hostility of these particular partisans was frightening. The priest went on to say how sad it was for me to die so young, adding that it was up to me to find a way out! So I asked him what he would suggest. At first he was quite uneasy but after a few seconds deliberating he said; "Your father is a rich man. If he would be prepared to pay 300,000 lire, I am sure we could arrange for your life will be spared."

I was speechless. He could see my reaction. In a rage I told him bluntly; "You will not get a penny from my father. I didn't do anything wrong and I am not going to sell my life. Now please leave me alone." He left the cell in silence. That was my death sentence! A few minutes later the chief partisan entered the cell and read a document to me. I did not hear much of what it said other than the fact that I was to be executed the following day.

Almost the entire population of the little town was waiting on the main street the next morning to say goodbye to me. People I had known most of my life waved sympathetically. Some of the women were crying. At that moment I felt like a *Povera Ricca Bambina* again. I was just twenty-four years old.

The guards marched me from the prison to the army barracks. It was the end of July and it was a glorious day "What a way to go," I thought. I tried to think about happy events and to recollect all the nice things that had happened to me until this moment. In the waiting room at the barracks, I was able to see my mother and my uncle for the last time. My dear mother was in great distress and her tears burned my soul. She was supported by my uncle, who was also tearful. I embraced them both and, at that point, I had to fight hard against my own inclination to weep like a child. But I was determined not to cry myself. My pride was too strong to let these people see my fear, even to the point of death. What was happening to me was a travesty of justice but it was also a time to show courage and to maintain my dignity. I had nothing to be ashamed of. I knew I was going to die, but I would die with a clear conscience.

The partisan chief led me into the barrack's yard and then on outside that yard to a short wall running at right angles to the main building. He turned me to place my back to the wall facing four partisans who were standing about five metres from us. They had machine-guns and I remember wondering how many shots they would fire to kill me. All of them were young men and I noticed that not one of them looked me in the eyes. I think they did not really relish the idea of killing me. I felt no resentment of them as they were only doing what they thought was their duty at the time. There was no sign of the chaplain. Not that I wanted to see him again as I think I would have spat at him.

The chief produced a blindfold from his coat pocket and tied it tightly around my head, covering my eyes, but the material of the blindfold was a bit threadbare and I could still see a bit of the ground through the bottom part of it. I was able to watch his feet as he moved away. I started to whisper a little prayer, a prayer I used to recite every night from the time I was a little girl. I still say that prayer to this day before I go to bed.

I seemed to wait a long time then. Perhaps it was just a sensation of time standing still because I knew they did nor normally wait too long to carry out the execution once the blindfold was in place. I waited to hear his commands to the firing squad that would end my life. My legs were starting to shake a bit by this time but I still fought to show no signs of fear.

Suddenly, instead of the chief's voice shouting orders, there was a commotion and I heard shouts from across the yard. Then silence. I was feeling numb. For what seemed like an eternity, but what was probably only a few seconds of more shouting and activity around me, somebody approached me and removed the blindfold. The sudden glare of sunlight blinded me for a moment.

When my eyes adjusted to the new light, the man I saw standing in front of me had a broad happy smile on his face. He was tall and handsome and when he spoke, his voice seemed to have a saintly, supernatural quality. No doubt I was in shock at the time but that man seemed to me to be a guardian angel sent by God to save me. "Do you recognise me?" he asked. I just shook my head dumbly. "Maybe you don't remember," he went on, "but I do, and I owe you my life." He took me by the arm and walked me past the chief partisan and the men with the machine guns. They stood back and did not interfere. I found out later that this new partisan chief was more senior to them in the *Brigate Garibaldine*. In truth, I did not have the faintest idea who he was or how I had managed to save his life but I was only too willing to return to the barracks with him.

My mother and my uncle were still there, waiting to take charge of my body! They could not believe their eyes to see me back alive. I still felt giddy, as if it was all a dream. I thought I would wake up at home, that I could vanish from this scene any minute! It took me a little while to realise that I was actually still alive! My mother started crying again. I started laughing, hysterically, I suppose. When we had calmed down a bit, my saviour explained to us how I had saved his life. It transpired that he was one of the hundreds of people who had received one of the Identity Cards from the *Kommandatur* during the war. The *Brigate Garibaldine* had their own intelligence network and they knew I was responsible for the issue of those cards! As soon as he heard of my impending execution, he rushed to the little town to stop the others from shooting me. Thank God he arrived just in time. Otherwise, I would not be telling my story now.

Unfortunately, the other partisans still insisted I was an enemy and they wanted to put me on trial as a collaborator. My saviour could not stop that, but he told me not to worry as the court would receive a letter from him explaining how I had helped him and other Italians from persecution by the SS. He explained that Italy was in a mood for revenge and anybody who had worked voluntarily for Mussolini's fascist regime or the Germans would be tried. I was safe from any real harm, he assured me, because the good I had done outweighed any bad. After an affectionate hug and kiss, he left me feeling quite happy for the first time since my arrest. In view of the fact that hundreds of people had already been summarily executed, including some women, I knew I was lucky even to get a trial.

On the way back to the town prison, people were still congregating on the main street. When they saw me alive, there were cheers and shouts of encouragement. A few of the women were sobbing. I will never forget that scene as long as I live.

I stayed in the town prison for another week but I was able to see my mother every day. One night, around midnight, I was woken and told to dress. I was taken by armed partisans to Vercelli, where my trial was to be held.

CHAPTER V

On the morning of August 27th 1945, I was standing at the bar in the Peoples Court of Justice in Vercelli, guarded by four carabinieri. The six judges, with red sashes over their black cloaks, came into the courtroom. "All stand," the court usher shouted. As the people stood, I looked around. My mother and my father were there. I was feeling glad to see them together again, even if it was not in happy circumstances. The hearing started.

After a few formal questions, the judges asked me if I knew what I was doing for two years as an interpreter in the German *Kommandatur*. My defence lawyer had advised me to say that I did not really know what I was doing for two years. I considered that to be a stupid defence. It was out of the question for me to answer in that way. How could I say that I did not know what job I did for two years?

"Your Honour," I replied, "I was always fully aware of my responsibility in trying to help people and to save lives to the best of my ability. I am proud of what I did." My lawyer gave me a nervous look when I finished.

There was a minute of silence, then the prosecutor, after a short summation that said nothing of the real circumstances of the case or the pressures of the war, proposed a four year prison sentence. There was no mention of any letter from my saviour. The court then retired to consider the matter without there being any submission from my lawyer other than a plea for clemency! While the judges were out, those friendly people who had come down for the trial from Varallo surrounded the bar to reassure me that the sentence was bound to be lenient.

However, as I found out later, behind the scenes, there was blackmail going on. These were lawless times and the partisans were a powerful force in Italy. They warned the judges that, if they did not dish out a severe sentence, they would all be shot! This was told to me by a sympathetic clerk of the court later when I was waiting to be moved to prison.

After one hour the judges returned. One of them read the sentence; "In the name of the people, you are sentenced to seven years and ten months." There was a brief silence and then gasps of dismay around the courtroom. I was shocked by the severity of the sentence. I felt like shouting out in protest at this injustice but I said, in as dignified a manner as I could, "Thank you Your Honours."

I then had a few minutes to say goodbye to my father and my mother, who was in tears, and to my friends before I was taken back to my cell. The Carabinieri were kind to me and took the trouble to assure me that there would soon be an Amnesty for all political prisoners convicted of less serious crimes. I felt I was innocent of any crime but I had to wait twelve long months for this amnesty to come into effect.

After the sentence, on September 28th 1945, I found myself back where I had started, in the hell that was Turin prison. By law, political prisoners were supposed to be kept separate from the common criminal convicts but, at this time, we were all kept together. The women's cells were on the first floor and the men were on the ground floor below us. There was a lot of sexist shouting going on every night between some of the women and their men-friends downstairs. An iron gate at the top of the stairs kept the sexes apart. It was not always effective because it was often unsupervised and, on occasions during the daytime, it was possible to observe a performance of 'the beast with two backs' by one of the women who was a member of the 'oldest profession'.

We also had to endure endless howling and shouting from women in the punishment cell. It was called *Il Buco* (the hole) because a large tin was suspended in the middle of the wire-mesh bed. This was supposed to take the place of a lavatory. Manacles were fixed at the top and bottom of the bed for each hand and

46

foot. The unfortunate victim had to lie down in chains for days!

Frequently, during the night, partisans came into the prison block to remove prisoners from the condemned cells for execution. They were shot against the prison walls. The general conditions were bad enough but the sound of those firing squads, sometimes preceded by hysterical howling or shouts of defiance from the condemned before the crashing sound of machine-gun fire brought a moment of silence throughout the prison, made this a fearful experience for me. They were desperately unjust times and, although many of those who were shot were probably guilty of serious offences, my own case gave me good reason to believe some of them were, like me, just innocent people caught up in the turmoil of war. I found it difficult to sleep and my nerves were frayed all the time I was in that dreadful place. Memories of Turin prison are firmly implanted on my brain.

However, being in prison in Turin had one advantage for me and for my parents. At least, we were in the same city. They could visit me for one half hour every week and they did not have to travel for two hours by train as before. Travelling by train was not very pleasant at that time.

On one of her visits, my mother gave me some very sad news. Our family's Jewish friends, Else and her son Alex, who, before the beginning of the war, lived in Turin, were nowhere to be found. Else's husband, Willy, was the son of an Italian tycoon. Alex was the same age as myself. After Willy died (she used to call him 'my sweet Willy') she decided to go back to Berlin with Alex to be with her family. Alex was a very nice, intelligent boy. His grandfather did not want him to leave Italy, especially for Germany where it was known Jews were being victimised. He wanted him, one day, to take over the business empire. But neither Else or Alex had been seen since they left Italy for Berlin. We could only assume they had become victims of the Nazi extermination policies, the full story of which was only then coming to light. I still have a photograph of Alex with me and some other girlfriends. We had a lovely time together and always remained good friends.

I started my sentence in cell-block N.7. Apart from the other difficulties, it was also very boring. There was only one half an hour's exercise each day in the yard. A few weeks after my arrival, however, we had more excitement than I wanted. The ordinary prisoners started a riot on the ground floor of the block. Their main aim was to break into the women's wing on the first floor where all the women political and common prisoners were being held. The army was alerted and soon the prison was surrounded by tanks.

The riot went on for three days and three nights. Thank God the men failed to break through the iron gate that separated the women's section. Then the shooting started. The noise and screaming was dreadful. Lots of the rioters were wounded and some of them were killed before the partisans regained control of the main prison on the ground floor. We had suffered for three days without food or sleep and, most of us, in deep fear.

After Christmas of 1946, we asked permission to give a performance in aid of charities. For several weeks we were busy organising and rehearsing a play called, *A Prison in a Prison.* Our relatives were allowed to donate costumes and props. I had to play the role of a smart old lady. My mother supplied two nice dresses, a pair of silk stockings and two pairs of shoes as well as some costume jewellery for my part. Wearing them made a refreshing change from the drab prison smocks.

A number of VIPs and dignitaries from Turin were invited to see the play. We put our hearts into the performance and it was received with a storm of applause from the audience. Many of the guests were very moved and came to shake hands with us afterwards.

I was still in my mother's clothes while escorting some of the guests to the main entrance. As my charges passed through the gate the guard standing there asked me if I had liked the

48

performance. She assumed I was one of the guests and was waiting for me to step outside. For a brief instant I was very tempted to walk through with my escorts. The thought of spending even one day outside that hell was almost overpowering but I knew it could not last and would only serve to make my eventual release that much more difficult. I stopped at the threshold and, with a wry smile on my face, I said to her; "You don't recognise me? I am one of the girls. Don't worry I am not running away." She nearly had a stroke! The expression on her face was one of pure astonishment and that started me laughing. She then slammed the gate shut and, glowering at me, pointed me back to the secure part of the prison.

By February 1946 talk about an amnesty was rife amongst the prisoners. Announcements were expected every day but, in the event, it took another four months before the first releases were initiated. In the meantime, most of the political prisoners, including myself, applied for work in one of the different industrial and occupational workshops in the prison. These had only just been opened up again after closure during the immediate post-war period. I went to a knitting and textiles workshop making clothes for women and babies I enjoyed this work and found that it eased the boredom and made the time pass more quickly.

In June 1946 the long awaited amnesty was declared. For political prisoners each trial was reviewed and, where the conviction was for crimes like minor 'collaboration' or simple membership of a fascist organisation, release was almost immediate. Those convicted of spying or informing on partisans, extortion or blackmail, and other more serious offences had their sentences reduced. Many were lucky not to have been shot.

At that time the word 'collaborator' still carried a serious stigma. Sentences were supposed to have been imposed according to the scale of involvement with the Germans. One girl among us had been sentenced to thirty years simply because her boyfriend was a leading fascist!

When I was finally released under amnesty, on July 5th 1946,

49

I left prison unrepentant. I regarded myself as innocent of any crime and very unjustly sent to prison. As I walked through the main gates to meet my mother outside I knew then that my year in prison was an experience I would never forget. The terrible memories have stayed with me to this day. Apart from the generally appalling conditions, the bad food and the sleepless nights we had to endure, the fearful time of the riot as the prisoners tried to get into the women's section and the subsequent bloodshed, the screams from the punishment cells and the dreadful sound of men being dragged to their execution had left an indelible mark upon my soul. I know that other women had been deeply affected by the experience because some of them had turned gray-haired before their time.

I know that such conditions no longer apply in our penal institutions these days, thank God, but I am always anxious when I hear people talking about life in prison being some sort of 'holiday' for the inmates. Repressive regimes in prison do nothing but instill hatred in the inmates. If they do not riot and injure prison staff or each other, they store that hatred until they are released and it may be some poor innocent who suffers from their blind revenge. I firmly believe that it is better to treat people in prison with respect and do whatever we can to reform their behaviour while they are under some kind of control.

CHAPTER VI

Naturally, after being confined in any sort of institution it takes a while to re-adjust to ordinary society. I had to learn again how to live a normal life. I went back to live with my mother in the same flat in Turin. My father and my brother had gone back to Milan.

I have not said very much about my brother, Filippo, up to now, but he was to become a source of much unhappiness for me later. He was ten years older than me and we had always lived apart. He had become an officer in the Italian army when the war began and he was taken prisoner with the Duca d'Aosta, a cousin of the King of Italy, while fighting in Ethiopia. He had just returned to Italy after five years in a British prisoner of war camp near Nairobi. The Duca d'Aosta died in captivity at the end of 1945 and was buried at the foot of Mount Kenya in a Mausoleum built by an Italian architect, Mario Rabaglino. Kenya was another country that, like Somalia, was to become an important part of my life later.

Everybody who remembers the post-war years will know life was not easy for most people. After my father's downfall, my mother succeeded in saving a lot of valuable jewellery and antiques. In an emergency she was very determined, very courageous and very efficient. It is a pity she did not teach my brother to be the same. She loved and spoiled him too much for his own sake. I, on the other hand, learned many things from her, probably because we were mother and daughter and had such a lot in common.

In those days of struggle to survive, it was difficult for me to find a job in Turin because of my having been 'on the wrong side' during the war. Too many people knew me, or of me, and whenever I went for a job interview somebody would recognise my name and remark on my 'collaboration'. Sometimes I met outright hostility and on other occasions apologetic excuses. It is remarkable how people, some of whom had actively supported the former regime, had become speedy converts after Italy was defeated and occupied.

Every interview I attended was followed by a letter declining to engage me in an capacity.

I realised I had to leave Turin if I was to make my own way in the world. Milan and Genoa were not options because I was known in those cities as well, So, one day, I told my mother it was time for me to leave home and go South to Rome. It was painful for us both but, after some discussion, she approved of my move. So, a couple of weeks later I packed by bags and took the long train journey to the Eternal City.

The Romans have a different individuality and a different outlook on life from other Italian city dwellers. The war did not seem to have affected them in the same way as it had affected people in the North. I found many jobs were available for those willing to work and I was always prepared to learn a new skill or about another trade. There is a saying in Italy: "Learn a job and put it aside. One day it will be useful."

My first job was in a beauty parlour where I learned a great deal about cosmetics and the latest beauty treatments. The pay was not very much but after a few months there I applied and was accepted as a counter clerk in a big travel agency. My ability in several languages was very helpful in getting this better paid work and I enjoyed my time there. By 1949 I wanted to extend myself a bit more. I had always been interested in fashion and, when the opportunity arose, I took a job in the most fashionable clothes store in the centre of Rome. My languages helped get that job as well because tourists formed a major section of the clientele. I was there for nearly two years and happy with my job, tough though it was. It was quite tiring standing on the shop floor for long hours.

One day I received a telephone call from a family friend. He was the chief of the War Graves Commission. He had located me through a mutual friend who visited the shop once as a customer. He told me that the German section of the Commission urgently needed somebody with good knowledge of the German language. I thanked him and fixed an appointment for the next day. I went to see my boss to tell him about the offer of the new job and asked if I had to give one month's notice. He was sorry to see me go because I was the only sales-girl in the shop who could speak foreign languages. However, he was very understanding. He accepted notice of one week and wished me all the best in my new job.

This was a fresh start and it took me back to the same occupation that had earned me a prison sentence, that of interpreter. However, this time I would be working for the Italian government, rather than the Germans, and with something new to learn. The War Graves Commission was part of the Ministry of Defence and it was concerned with finding the burial sites of Italian soldiers who had died in battles throughout Italy and re-interring their bodies in several war cemeteries. At first I was helping to establish a card-index of the dead and a record of the location of their graves. It was a long, painful task, and a duty, to put to rest all the brave ones who lost their lives for their country.

One morning I saw a note on the office notice-board asking for a volunteer to help repatriate dead Italian soldiers from Germany. I asked about it from one of my colleagues in the section. He told me the notice had been on the board for the past two weeks but nobody had come forward yet as the job was regarded as somewhat gruesome. I said to myself "somebody has to do it," and so I went to see the Chief the same day. He asked me if I was happy in my job on the third floor.

"Yes thank you," I replied, "I only came to see if the job as a volunteer was still available."

"It is unbelievable." he exclaimed. "After two weeks nobody has come forward yet. I don't think this is a job for a girl, even if your knowledge of the German language would be very useful."

"Sir," I replied, "you just give me the chance, please. Give me two months and I will come back to you to report."

He smiled. "Very well," he said.

One year passed and all went well for me in my new job. Myself and two employees of the MOD had the task of meeting the grieving relatives of the deceased soldiers on the spot where they were buried; sometimes a cemetery, sometimes in a grove or a field, anywhere were the unfortunate casualties of war were buried. We drove from site to site in a black Fiat van that could carry ten coffins. A black cross on the roof and an inscription on each side in Italian, French and English stated our function and we frequently met with the 'sign of the cross' from people we passed travelling around the country.

Nearly every day we had appointments with the relatives in different towns and places. My job was to provide the mayor of the town or area with all the information about the name of the deceased and the day the grave should be prepared for the exhumation to take place. At every appointment the back door of the van was covered with the Italian flag and there were two big flower vases and two high candlesticks to stand on the ground during the ceremony. I read a prayer during the disinterment and sometimes the relatives gave me a little souvenir to put in the coffin. It was nearly always heartbreaking to witness the distress of mothers and relatives during these rituals. It was not, however, always straight-forward.

The worst incident happened on the Swiss-German border during one of our journeys. We arrived at the border in the afternoon, planning to be in Fallinbostel in the evening to be ready for the next day's exhumation

At the German frontier checkpoint, instead of taking down the chain and letting us through, the customs officer ordered us to leave the van and enter the office. They asked who spoke German. I was the only German speaker and so they started to question me.

In the meantime two other officers were checking the van. The doors and the inside were taken to pieces and all the coffins put outside and opened. In the end, I was feeling very exasperated and I asked him what they were looking for.

"Drugs," was the reply!

54

I was frantic and tried to convince the officer we had no drugs in the van. He told me that a black van, exactly like ours, passed through the border two days before us and they had received a warning from the Swiss about drug smuggling in a black van.

We parted friends in the end, but we missed the last ferry and had to stay overnight in Konstanz. The Customs paid for our hotel but we were late for our appointment the next day. The van was in a mess and had to be repaired.

Because of the Customs search of the van the previous day the lock on the door near the passenger seat was not working. We had not had the time to repair it and so, for three days, I had to keep the door closed with a piece of rope wrapped around my wrist while the driver kept casting anxious glances at me to make sure he did not lose me when we went around bends.

On another journey we arrived very late at a place called Paderborn because the van broke down. We had to be ready for another exhumation the following day. The two men engaged to dig up the grave agreed to do the repairs to the van in the evening but the delay meant that we were still in the cemetery after midnight to complete the exhumation.

My travelling companion looked at his watch and then said to me: "I'll bet you are the only woman in the world doing this job at midnight!"

Our next trip was to Berlin which, at that time, was divided in three sectors. We had a permit to enter the French and English sectors, but not the Russian sector. The Russian sector was separated by a barbed wire fence with searchlight and machine-gun positions. We had to pass the checkpoint gates and its wires in the dark. We switched off the lights of the van and managed to drive away between the searchlights to make sure we were not shot at.

Our next assignment was in Gottingen, where we had to perform a very difficult and gruesome exhumation. We first had to identify the bodies, each of which was buried in a black nylon bag. Some were without skulls. The corpses were still decomposing and we had to use the normal coffins instead of the small ones. On this occasion we were forced to use the surgical masks with which we were equipped. That was a very unpleasant part of the job.

On our way back home we stopped at Dachau, the notorious Nazi concentration camp. At that time only foreigners had permission to visit the camp which had, by then, been converted into one huge garden. But all the signs of the horrors that had taken place there were still to be seen. The scale and nature of such inhumanity should never be forgotten.

CHAPTER VII

When this part of the Commission's work was done I returned to the office routine back in Rome. One day, in 1950, I was leaving the office when a man approached me downstairs at the entrance.

"Hello," he said with a big smile. "Maybe you don't remember me. I am Franco, a friend of your brother."

His name was familiar and, as I scrutinised his face, memory of him came back to me. Just more than four years earlier, in 1945, he and my brother had returned together from a POW camp in Kenya. I remembered meeting him a couple of times with my brother in Turin after I was released from prison in 1946.

"I spoke to your mother and she told me you were working in Rome. She gave me your office address." he went on.

"So," I asked, "What brings you here?" I was puzzled.

He smiled shyly. "I couldn't forget you and I wanted to see you again. Could we meet somewhere?"

I was very flattered and I did not want to hurt him by refusing. So we arranged to meet next day, in the afternoon, at the Babington Tea-rooms near the Spanish Steps.

We became good friends. He was kind and was always ready to give me good advice when needed. He was still living in Turin but often came to Rome for business reasons.

One day, in October, he asked me, to my surprise, "Will you marry me?" and quickly added, "Next month I am going to Somalia to open an office for Import Export in Mogadishu with a partner who is a friend of mine. We could get engaged now and next spring we could get married."

When he mentioned Somalia, a lot of memories came flooding back to me. My father, my uncle! I never thought that fate would take me there one day. I asked him to give me a little time before I gave him my answer.

It was not love on my side, but more of affection and the need to have a man whom I could trust, someone to lean on in my difficult life. At that time I was working hard. One job with the Commission at their offices in the morning and two other jobs, in the afternoon and evening, as a translator. I had to work hard because I was supporting my mother.

The next time we met at the Babington Tea-rooms, we became engaged. We had a small party with a few friends and the next day Franco left for Mogadishu. The following months went very fast and on my 30th birthday, I left Brindisi on board the *Lloyd Triestino*.

Jerusalemme! Destination Mogadishu. We got married on the first day of June in 1951. It was a simple ceremony performed by the Bishop of Mogadishu and attended by the Italian community. A telegram arrived from the Pope and from Cascais from the King of Italy in exile.

Maria, my husband's sister, was also present at the wedding. She was the only representative from either family. She has always been like a real sister to me and I am very grateful to her for her loving understanding throughout many years.

Nine days after the wedding I started work at the statistics office of the Italian A.F.I.S. (*Amministrazione Fiduciaria Italiana Somalia*) to be able to continue to support my mother. I did not want to involve my husband with any extra financial burden as it was something I felt I had to do.

Our first home, near the Mosque, was a small bungalow with a tiny sunken garden that looked like a swimming pool during the rainy season. We had a *boiessa* (housegirl) called Gurgushu. She was a Christian and she was often drunk. When my husband was on safari, I use to keep a *bilau* (a sort of hunting knife) under my pillow at night, in case she tried to smuggle in her boyfriend. In the end I sacked her. The next housegirl we had was a Muslim and, then, I could not keep a piece of ham in the fridge!

Our next home was built in the Arab style and it was called 'The Sheik's House'. I loved it. Mogadishu, at that time, was a lovely town with lovely buildings, an ancient cathedral, beautiful shops, good hotels and restaurants. We had a busy social life and regularly attended the Italian Club, the Tennis Club, and the Yacht Club. All the natives had jobs and were happy and contented and most of them spoke Italian. Only the weather was a problem. It was very hot, especially during *Tangabili*, the hottest season of the year.

I used to visit my uncle Giuseppe's grave and the cotton plantations with the cotton mill, that once belonged to my father. But there was nothing left by then, just a mountain of rubble! Every single building had been destroyed.

Now in Somalia there seems to be only war, misery and famine. Where are all the beautiful Somali women with their colourful dresses and glittering gold and all the lovely little children? I cry when I see the terrible sights of Somalia on the television these days.

Not long after our arrival in Mogadishu I had become aware that Franco was partial to Somali women. During the war in Ethiopia he had spent his leave in Mogadishu. Somali women are famous for their beauty and I had a chance to meet some of his female 'acquaintances' at the Italian restaurant in the city. They had complemented him on his marriage and made remarks about how lucky he was to have such an attractive wife! I did not realise then that he was still having liaisons with some of them but it did not take too long before I became aware of the hurtful truth. It became an issue between us and a cause of unhappiness and concern for me.

After four years, my husband decided it was time to make a change. He had grown up in a family of hoteliers. As a young boy he went to Hotel School and, with experience in several hotels abroad and knowledge of five languages, he was looking for a post as a hotel manager.

He got the job he wanted in one of the most beautiful places in the world, in the Limuru district of the Kenyan Highlands, about twenty-five miles from Nairobi. I was quite happy to leave Mogadishu because I thought it would make a difference to our marriage relationship. I was wrong.

It was 1954. After the sandhills and semi-deserts of Somalia, the Kenyan Highlands looked like a real paradise! The Brackenhurst Hotel, surrounded by thirty-six acres of land and gardens, including an eighteen hole golf course, was a dream! There were forty-three cottages scattered around the lawns of the main building which included the dining-room, three lounges, kitchen, stores and offices. Opposite was the main bar and a billiard room. There were seventy-six rooms but only half of them were in use. The others were all 'out of order.' Every time one of the rooms needed maintenance the previous manager had just locked the door and thrown the keys into a shoebox in the manager's office. It was there that I found them. It was also then that I realised my marriage was a mistake.

When a husband and wife are working together, problems will always arise that cause arguments. My husband came from a Catholic family but he had a Muslim mentality and a Muslim inclination. He knew the Koran by heart and one of his languages was Arabic, which he spoke fluently. He was a workaholic and a perfectionist. All of this, combined with his frequent philandering trips back to Mogadishu over the course of the next several years, did not help to make me happy.

When we took over the management of the hotel, I did not speak English or Swahili. My husband put me in charge of the catering and said to me, in effect; "You are on your own. Sorry I can't help you, I am far too busy!" and that was all there was to it.

We had a fairly large staff that included; carpenters, plumbers, decorators, builders, electricians and tailors as well as

60

the ordinary catering workers. Just for the gardens, we had twenty five shamba boys (gardeners). The first year was very difficult for me. I tried hard to learn to speak English and I practised in the reception with the two English receptionists and with the hotel guests. One day a guest was telling me how much she enjoyed the horse races in Nairobi. "Oh!" I said, "Have you vet a horse?" She was so amused that, from that day, she started to give me English lessons in my free time. I have never forgotten her kindness and I will always be grateful to her.

Reading books and newspapers was also a big help, but it took me one year to be able to hold a conversation or to read and write English as a beginner. I also needed to learn Swahili. It was very important and necessary for me to get through to the African staff in order to be able to understand them when we working together. It took me only three months to learn Swahili well enough for the purpose.

The most urgent job, besides the catering, was to restore all the rooms not in use. I had to start this task by myself, at first without the assistance of a housekeeper. Then later, with the help of an Italian housekeeper, Gianna, we made the disused seventy five rooms ready. She was great. A very hard working and a very good friend. She died in Italy some years later. I will never forget her. Thank you Gianna!

In the following months we built a village for the hotel staff and for the sixty *totos* (children). I opened a school for the children in one of the old cottages with a *mwalimu* (teacher) in charge to teach English and Swahili. I bought yards of green Jinja cotton and the hotel's tailor made a uniform for each of them. It was nice to see them coming down the hill singing, two by two and dressed in the green uniform, to start school in the morning. They looked like little Kermit! We also built a social hall, with a record-player for the staff, where they had dance competitions and New Year's parties. It was all hard work but with plenty of satisfaction.

61

In the years to come, we built a new wing for all of the six international airlines whose crews would stay for the week-end or for longer breaks. Twice a month we had American tours and even President Johnson came once to play golf. Also the German Chancellor, Herr Willy Brandt, came with his wife for a week's holiday. Both had special security guards.

The hotel had a very good reputation for *haute cuisine*. For the gourmets, truffles were flown in from Italy by Alitalia. Every Sunday we use to serve 350 lunches and 450 teas. The golf course had a night-club event every Saturday when salmon and caviar would be served at midnight to the music of a band from Nairobi. Every year in January there was the Hunt Club Ball and the Scottish Society's Party and at Easter the 'Hillclimb' car competition was held.

Many Italian people came from Mogadishu to the hotel for holidays. I was always pleased to see them but, on one occasion, I was put in a very difficult situation. I went to the airport to meet a lady with her sister who, I noticed, was pregnant. I asked her how many months, "nearly nine," she said laughing. "Didn't the airline notice?" I asked. "I just kept my coat in front of me." she said still laughing. I told her that it could be quite risky and dangerous and just hoped for the best. A few days later I was awakened in the middle of the night by the frightened and terrified sister. The lady had started labour. At that time my husband was away attending the Independence Celebrations in Mogadishu .

I was alone and I had to act quickly. We were twenty five miles from Nairobi and there were no ambulances. I put a mattress with pillows and blankets in the back of the hotel station-wagon for the patient to lie on and, with the hotel driver and the distressed woman's sister, we drove to a nursing home down the road. It was already three in the morning. When we arrived, the matron was drunk!. Luckily a room was free and the African nurse helped me to put the lady to bed. I tried to contact the local doctor but he was also drunk! After two hours it didn't look good. The pains were more and more frequent. Then I decided to call my own doctor in Nairobi. I explained the case to him and begged him to come as soon as possible. He promised to be there in half an hour. Thank God for that because it was a very difficult delivery. The doctor told me that in another two hours mother and child could have died. He took the lady in his car to Nairobi and promised to ring as soon as possible. In the meantime I went back to the hotel with the sister to have a few hours sleep. The doctor rang me the next day in the afternoon with the good news.:- mother and child were fine. It was a girl! "You saved both their lives," he told me. Two more hours and it would have been too late. I was so happy and relieved. After three days the lady with the baby, a lovely girl, came back to the hotel. The husband had just arrived from Mogadishu to take her home. He was very apologetic, and grateful.

By 1955 Kenya was awakening to a sad reality. A dangerous political situation, simmering for some time, was going to explode at any moment. The Kikuyu tribe all over Kenya (the Mau-Mau Party) were seeking freedom from British rule and were ready to fight. Their leader, Jomo Kenyatta, was near the end of his long imprisonment in Maralal. The freedom fighters were gathering deep in the forests all over Kenya ready to start a war campaign. One of the chiefs, in the Limuru area, was Danti Kimathi. The Brackenhurst Hotel was in the middle of the fight! However, we still had a lot of tourists and local residents who were not frightened off.

It all started one day just before the arrival of a party of Americans. Three lorries from the Tigoni police station arrived with ten policemen who quickly assembled all the Kikuyu staff, leaving behind only the other tribes; Wakamba, Kipsigis and Jalou. An internment camp at Voi, on the Mombasa road, was the destination for the Kikuyu. We were left with just one third of the staff, the two English receptionists and a fifteen year old messenger boy.

When the American party arrived, they quickly noticed that

something was wrong. The tour leader said to me "You having trouble with the staff?" I did not want to be an alarmist and, with a smile and a reassuring shake of the head, I started to direct the luggage to the scattered cottages around the hotel grounds. The freedom fighters were hiding in the forest near the Mabrukie Tea Estate which lay behind the Hotel, so every day we had incursions by the police searching the grounds. They used to inform us every time in advance, so we had time to take the residents' children away from the playground. Early one morning we were awakened by a heavy knock at our cottage door. Our upset *shamba* boy (gardener) told us to come quickly to the vegetable garden. When I got there I was deeply shocked to see the bodies of two African policemen lying there in the cauliflower beds. They had been decapitated. I will never forget that sight. For one year afterwards I could never eat cauliflower!

Such excitements soon became a regular feature of our daily life. My husband bought two revolvers for our own protection and I was obliged to practise at an improvised shooting range. Tourists were beginning to become scarce because of the activities of the Mau-Mau who, by then, had started attacking isolated plantations and killing British people.

There were many other brutal and tragic events that affected us before the emergency was over. A dining-room waiter was killed coming down from the staff quarters on his way to work one morning in the early hours. Mwangi was a good worker, spoke good English and was one of the best waiters in the hotel. They killed him and took one shilling that he had in his pocket. I heard him screaming for help but, by the time I got there with my husband and other members of the staff he was already dying from stab wounds. We could do nothing to save him and I just cradled him in my arms while he died a couple of minutes later. Another waiter, Kamau, was on his way back to the staff quarters one evening with a parcel of leftovers from the kitchen. He was strangled with his *mushipi* (the red belt worn over the white shirt) and the parcel of leftovers was taken by his killers.

Limuru was a beautiful landscape and it looked like the English countryside. We knew all the farmers who supplied fresh provisions to the hotel. One elderly lady would supply us with fresh eggs every day. Mwaniki, the store boy, told me the lady had not come that morning. I was very surprised. She was always very punctual. I sent an *askari* (a hotel security guard) down to her farm and he came back with terrible news. The poor lady was found dead in her bed with her head cleaved. We found out later that her houseboy had taken the Mau-Mau oath the night before. The oath required them to swear to kill the first white person they met the next morning. Instead of bringing her the early morning *chai* (tea) he had slashed her head. Only the day before the lady had given him a present of a bicycle and a *kanga* (a roll of dress material) for his wife.

Next was a little British boy. One morning he was on his bicycle in the garden when the houseboy came through the gate. He greeted him, "*Jambo, Mwangi*". He had known him since he was born. Mwangi took out a *panga* (machete) from under his *kansus* (long shirt) and slashed the boy's head killing him instantly. The boy's mother was only a few yards away but could do nothing to prevent the outrage. The situation became very tense all over the country from then on.

One morning we had a surprise visitor. On our doorstep was a beautiful Alsatian dog lying in a pool of blood with a look of pain in his eyes. It was a police dog who had been working with the homeguard chasing the Mau-Mau. The terrorists had slashed his right leg with a panga. I put him in the lounge of our cottage on a blanket near the log fire and rang the Tigoni Vet. He cleaned the wound and stitched up the skin. We could not trace the original owner or handler to establish his name so we called him Fido, meaning somebody faithful, trustworthy. After one month Fido was right as rain! I was glad of his company, especially when I had to go about the hotel grounds at night. I felt safe with him and my gun. If the staff wanted to know where I was they had only to look for Fido.

A few months later we had an American film company staying at the Hotel. The son of the cameraman was fifteen years old. He was a troublemaker. Because it was a public place, I had to keep Fido tied up near our cottage during the day. That boy started inciting the other residents' children to tease Fido whenever I was not there. They would throw stones at him and threaten him with sticks.

One evening when he was free around the gardens, Fido recognised his tormentor and bit the boy on his arm. So, that was it! The boy's father threatened to sue us and I had to give up my best friend! I sent Fido to a farm ten miles away that belonged to a friend of mine. It was not too far for me to go to see him when I wished but it was terribly sad to see Fido sitting near the driver in the hotel station-wagon as they left for his new home.

After one week my friend rang me. She sounded very distressed; "Gemma, Fido has disappeared!" I was worried sick that somebody might have killed him. We went down the road several times looking for him. Next day a shamba boy came to me *"Memsahib Fido ku-isha rudi!"* (Fido is back). I ran down the road and there he was! Walking slowly, hungry and tired, but happy to see me. It was a tearful reunion. In the meantime the film company had already left and the other children were strictly warned not to tease him again. At last, I had Fido back with me again and safe.

It was 1956 and we were still in the middle of the Mau Mau uprising. However, with Fido again at my side, I was feeling a little bit safer. However, with just a few of the hotel's Askaris and Kipsigi tribesmen armed only with spears, it was still not very reassuring. At that time, we were really in God's hands! I believe now that our Italian nationality saved us from any of the direct murderous attacks

66

that were being directed at British people.

Nevertheless, there were occasional funny episodes to break the general air of tension. Because of the long rainy season, which led to some soil subsidence, a large hole appeared in the floor of the hotel billiard room, near the entrance door, and it became dangerous due to its depth. The workmen put railings around it with a light in the middle as a warning sign. One late evening a police officer, after a few beers, did not see the warning light and fell down the hole. He was furious when the barman helped him out and he demanded to see the manager. My husband was away on a 'trip' to Mogadishu at the time and I was awakened by several knocks on the door of the cottage accompanied by loud shouting. Fearing it was a Mau Mau attack, I grabbed my gun and, very nervous, started shouting back, "*Basta, basta!*" as I went to the door. My heart was pounding madly and I pointed my revolver at the door. I could not make out what was being shouted but it continued even more furiously along with the banging on the door. I, in turn, was shouting, "*Basta! basta!*" at whoever was on the other side. When I finally realised it was not terrorists, I opened the door to find the policeman standing there. He immediately started shouting at me, "You have called me a bastard, I am a police officer and that is an offence. You are under arrest!" He thought I had been calling him a bastard! I tried to calm him down and to explain to him that in Italian 'basta' means 'stop'. When the penny dropped he calmed down. He muttered something about 'foreigners' and went away, rather embarrassed. He did not even mention the hole he had fallen into and, when I saw him the next day, he was very apologetic about the incident. He might have been a bit less embarrassed and apologetic if he had known how close I came to firing my gun through the door!

Towards the end of 1956 the political situation in Kenya began to be more stable and negotiations were initiated for the independence of Kenya between the English Government and Jomo

Kenyatta. Since we had not had a holiday for years, we could now leave the hotel for a few days. We decided to visit South Africa on a cruise-ship with some friends, a married couple called Farrant. They were lovely people and they had two nice teenage boys. We left Mombasa in the middle of September and sailed down the East Coast of Africa to Dar-es-Salaam, Lorenzo Marques, Durban, East London, Port Elizabeth and finally to Cape Town.

It was the cold season. On our arrival in Cape Town harbour, the ship was surrounded by lots of seals. We had a lovely time. We went up to the top of Table Mountain to enjoy the magnificent view out over the city and the bay. We walked along Adderley Street, famous for its many jewellery shops with their fantastic diamonds on display. We also fed the squirrels, which is a well known tourist pastime in the city. Outward bound on the ship we had also become friendly with another passenger, Mrs Zwickau, who invited us to her vineyard near Paarl in the Cape. That was a lovely day out. We had an equally enjoyable, relaxing, time on the return voyage to Mombasa.

Back in Brackenhurst a letter was waiting for me. The family lawyer in Italy gave me the sad news that my uncle, Eugenio, who had shared the villa in Varallo with my mother and me during the war, was paralysed in hospital. He was seventy-two years old and he wanted to see me. I was surprised he did not call my mother and my brother, who, at that time were living in Vienna.

So I was going back to my dear old home in the little town full of memories. I had left it convinced I would never see it again! When I arrived after a long flight, I travelled straight to the hospital. My uncle was delighted to see me. The family lawyer was in the room with him. When my grandmother died, she left the entire estate to uncle Eugenio. Now he wanted to name me as his heir. He was sure the estate would not be squandered and that I would do my best to keep it in the family. I assured him, grateful for the trust he gave me, that I would do so. The lawyer had the will prepared and we signed it together with two witnesses from the hospital. I reassured my uncle I would stay at the villa until he was able to return home. That made him so happy! He was a wonderful painter and etcher. He was well known in Italy and for many years he taught at the Albertina Academy in Genova. He told me to take some of his etchings of Genova, my birthplace, back to Nairobi with me and also to take whatever else I would like. I took two small snow landscapes of his. All are still with me and they will always be treasured.

When my grandfather, Giovanni, retired to Italy, the Italian Government asked him once if he would open the villa with all the collections in it, to the public. At that time it was a very uncommon thing to happen and certainly not when the owner was still alive. I was always fond of my uncle Chicai (Eugenio)) the painter. I was the only one who was allowed in his studio, sitting in silence behind him, fascinated, during his painting and etching. He use to teach me many useful things and to love art and nature and the composition and arrangement of colours. He was a great artist and was also a wonderful pianist. He never married but he had a life of his own.

My other uncle, Bepi (Giuseppe), the sculptor, had a very unhappy marriage and went away to Somalia. He died there in 1927. I was only a young child when I saw him but I will remember him always as the man with the gentle smile.

I stayed at the villa nearly one month and enjoyed every day of it, strolling through the forest and around the gardens with Leda, a lovely watchdog, and met all my old friends. When my uncle came home from hospital it was time for me to leave for Nairobi, but not before I had organised a permanent nurse and the help of Maria, the old housekeeper with thirty-eight years of service, as well as the help of the gardener and his wife, the cook. I left with peace of mind, knowing that he was well cared for.

Before I left I also said good bye to our ghost! Yes! We had a ghost! I had been sleeping in my grandmother's room since I arrived. Every night while I was there I was awakened by light footsteps outside the door. After the first night I mentioned the phenomena to Maria. She asked me if it could have been my grandmother, Margarethe? I could not answer positively because all I heard was footsteps but I had a strong feeling of well-being when I heard them and I was convinced it was my loving grandmother returning to keep an eye on things while my uncle was in hospital. Bless her soul. I will never know!

I left my uncle happy in his home and went back to Kenya and the Brackenhurst Hotel happier for the break. I resumed my usual routine. The following year, 1957, the family lawyer wrote to me again to let me know that my brother and my mother had left Vienna because of the news of my uncle's stroke. They were now looking after him and had settled in the villa permanently. The lawyer asked me if I was prepared to return to Italy. I knew I was at a crossroads in my life but I could not easily decide to leave Nairobi for an indefinite period of time, specially when I had always tried in the past to avoid living with my brother again.

My uncle died suddenly a month or so later. I received my brother's telegram, just a few words to let me know of uncle's death. The lawyer's letter followed shortly afterwards. With his condolences he gave me the news: my brother was the only heir to the estate, including the entire contents of the villa. The lawyer told me my uncle's will had been changed a few weeks before his death. I only hoped his death was a peaceful one. I was devastated and I will always remember my best uncle, the only one that never failed to bring me sweets every Sunday in the whole seven years I was in the convent in Genova.

In the same year I experienced a happier event, the birth of my god-daughter, Marina, on April 25th 1957. Marina's mother and father, Teresa and Sergio Daros, were Italians who lived in Nairobi. When Teresa was expecting, I told her that if the baby was a girl I would like to be her godmother. Sure enough, one day

Sergio rang me: "Gemma, it's a girl! From today you are a godmother!" My god-daughter is now happily married with a good husband, Carlo. They have a bright and clever son, Gianluca.

The years went by. In 1959 we met our new neighbours, Carlo and Olga Quaglia, and we became very good friends. They had the Tigoni Farm, one of the best dairy farms in the country with a herd of thirty-five Jersey cows. It was in the Limuru Hills just ten minutes drive from Brackenhurst and situated in a beautiful landscape with a lovely South African style mansion where I spent many happy hours.

One day Carlo and Olga had a very distinguished visitor, the Countess Edda Ciano, the eldest daughter of Mussolini. She was a remarkable lady, dedicated to her country. She worked for the Red Cross during the war in Albania and Russia. She was a strong character, very courageous, and she was much respected and admired. In spite of the fact that she was the dearest daughter of Mussolini, she defied her father and her life held a terrible destiny. She never forgave her father for not having saved the life of her husband. "I am proud of him." she declared the day Count Galeazzo Ciano was shot as a traitor after the Verona trial on January 11th 1944. Her life ended that day! She had written to her father: "I bear the blood-stained name of my husband with pride." She died in Rome in 1995 at age of eighty-five years. I will always remember her at the dinner party we gave for her before she left Kenya.

With most of the hard work done at the hotel getting the unused rooms back into service, I found myself with a bit of spare time on my hands. Some local children were attending dance classes and I approached the organiser to enquire if I could open a ballet class. The idea was gladly accepted and so I started to teach the class on two afternoons every week. It gave me an opportunity to practice for myself and to listen to the music I had always found enchanting. The children thoroughly enjoyed the class and I carried this on for a couple of years.

Tigoni Farm, in the beautiful Limuru Hills.

The main building of the Brackenhurst Hotel.

Photograph taken soon after I arrived in Kenya in 1954.

74

In my ballet outfit during one of the classes.

75

Photographs taken during a visit to the Masai Reserve in Kenya.

CHAPTER VIII

It was 1960. Regrettably, a year of changes. After all the hard work, in difficult times, to bring Brackenhurst back to its previous splendour, my husband, always keen to go to new places, decided to accept an offer to manage the Imperial Hotel in Kampala. It was a great sadness for me to have to leave behind all that I had worked for and grown to love.

It would be our last Christmas in Brackenhurst and it was time for me to organise the various functions of the season. The New Year Dinner and Dance was held in the main dining room with a band from Nairobi. My friend, Rosetta from Riararidge Farm, was helping me. Rosetta may well remember this occasion with pleasure but for me personally, this happy affair was tinged with sadness because it was to be my last big event at Brackenhurst.

The children's party started, as always, in the bright sunshine of the afternoon with Father Christmas riding a white horse down the hill through the golf course with two little donkeys following behind loaded up with bags of presents. All the parents were waiting with cameras to take pictures of their excited children wearing their party dresses. It was a real pleasure to watch them opening their presents under the Christmas tree. The hotel's two cooks were in attendance to serve the children their special menu.

After so many years the time came to say goodbye to all our staff in the social hall at the last party. I wept, they wept! *"Memsahib, hapana ku-enda!"* (Madam, don't go!). It was the first time I had seen Africans really crying. It was even more painful to have to leave behind all our many very good friends who have remained so ever since. Also, the owner of Brackenhurst, Toby Block of Block Hotels, and his family, I will always remember with deep fondness. I was saddened to hear of his death recently.

Then it was time to leave Brackenhurst for our new

destination in Uganda. But even there I encountered trouble because, in the neighbouring countries of Rwanda and Burundi, then part of the Belgian Congo, a nationalist rebellion was going on against the Belgians.

We were just taking over the management of the Imperial Hotel in Kampala, when the exodus of Belgian settlers began. It was a sad and terrifying sight to see. Every day streams of refugees from the Belgian colonies passing through the centre of town, with all their belongings which they tried to sell. You could buy a nearly new car for as little as one thousand Uganda Shillings. Many other items of property could also be bought for very little because the settlers were desperate to raise money to get back to Europe. Many of them were slaughtered before they had a chance to escape.

Army units from various countries were sent to the Belgian Congo under the United Nations to defend the white settlers who tried to flee from the Tutzi and Hutu tribes. One day a mission of eleven Italian officers arrived at the Imperial to stay the night. They were on their way to Kigali. I arranged a private dining-room for them and provided them each with an unexpected and welcome plate of spaghetti! In the brief time they were at the hotel we became very friendly with them. They left the next morning saying, "*Arrivederci*". They were planning to return to Kampala after a one week tour. Not one of them ever came back! On their arrival in Kigali barracks they were slaughtered in the officer's mess having been mistaken for Belgian army personnel. We heard later that their bodies were dismembered and sold in the local market, together with their uniforms. An Italian military aircraft went there to fly the bodies to Italy, but all the coffins went back empty, mercifully, without the knowledge of the families. The oldest officer, the captain, was thirty-three years old! I was so shocked by this news that I left the hotel for three days and went to stay with two dear friends, Giuliana and Domenico, with their little daughter

78

Dianella, at Masaka. I really needed to go away for a time.

All the refugees were directed to Nairobi in Kenya to wait for flights to take them back to Belgium. My friend, Olga, kindly offered accommodation to a Belgian lady with two children. When they left one week later, Olga was horrified and very disappointed when she found the condition in which they had left the two lovely rooms with antique furniture which she had provided for them.

In 1962 an opportunity arose for me to do something different. It was a coincidence to meet Dennis Lloyd and his wife again, this time at the reception desk of the Imperial Hotel. They had been residents with us at the Brackenhurst at the time Dennis was the manager of East African Airways in Nairobi. Now he was being transferred to the East African Airways office in Kampala. He asked me if I was happy in the new place. The Imperial was very different from Brackenhurst which I was missing very much. I told him I was not so enthusiastic about my new place and he asked me if I would like to work for East African Airways in Kampala. I did not have any specific job in the hotel at that time so I accepted the offer. It was another new job for me and I was sure I would enjoy it. Dennis and the sales manager, John McLoughlin, were very helpful and so were all the staff. I started in the booking office with one of the girls. She was very good and patient with a beginner like me. My languages came in useful especially for escorting the tourists in the various Game Parks. By this time my English was pretty good thanks to my time and lessons at Brackenhurst.

Uganda became independent from Britain that same year and VIPs were gathering from all over the world for the Independence Celebrations. The owner of the Imperial Hotel, Count Kassim Lakka, was the head of the Ismaili community in East Africa. He was a member of the Aga Khan's family. He also owned the Oceanic Hotel in Mombasa. He was a real gentleman with a lovely family. His daughter, Karim Kassim Lakka, owned a very *chic* boutique in the centre of Nairobi, 'Sakuntala', from which I still have some beautiful trouser-suits.

The more prominent guests were the Aga Khan with the Begum, the Duke of Kent, representing the Queen, the Prime Minister of Israel, Mrs Golda Meir, the Kenyan President, Jomo Kenyatta, and many more. Mr Milton Obote was to be appointed President of Uganda. One evening was dedicated to the performance of traditional dances, costumes and music. On the day of Independence the hotel name changed! From now on it would be The Grand Hotel. The independence celebrations lasted nearly a week.

The following year, 1963, was the year Kenya became independent. The British Government started negotiations to bring out English settlers in order to return the land to the native people. A big change was already under way. A sad change for many but probably necessary for the peace of the country. Anyway, we were ready again for another change ourselves.

I loved my job in the airline and I was very sorry to have to leave East African Airways, the management and other colleagues had all become very good friends. Our next destination was Tanzania. My husband got an offer from AGIP to start an AGIP Motel in Dar-es-Salaam.

The building was nearly completed. Only the interiors had to be organised. It was quite a task but it was the sort of challenge that made Franco accept the offer with enthusiasm. In the meantime, the Italian Embassy in Dar-es-Salaam was looking for a secretary to organise the Ambassador's office. He had just arrived from Italy. I had an interview in his office and I started work immediately. I was to work in the administration department with a colleague, Vera Mannini. We got on well together and became good friends. I settled down happily in my new job. It was a job that needed to be organised in many branches, confidential and in a trustworthy manner, and always with a diplomatic touch.

Oyster Bay was the most fashionable quarter in Dar-es-Salaam where all the diplomatic missions had their residences. The Italian Residence was a Spanish villa with a lovely garden and an artistically designed ceramic tiled pond. I organised dinner parties and entertained guests in Italian style around the pond.

We had the best Italian Club in East Africa. It was a lovely building with a sea view, swimming-pool, ballroom, lawn-tennis court and a table tennis area. It was built by an Italian architect and, every Saturday, the Italian community would gather for entertainment and for special functions. Every Sunday we spent time with friends and with my god-daughter's family at a lovely beach with a small bungalow called Cadaval. In the evening we would all meet at the Italian Club. We had a really good time, but it was not to be forever. An eruption was simmering beneath the apparent calm.

It was October 1965 and suddenly we found ourselves in the middle a full mutiny of the Tanzanian Army. My husband used to take me in the car to my job at the Embassy every morning before going on to the Agip Motel. One morning in the centre of town we noticed a strange movement of army vehicles. They were full of armed soldiers and loaded with other heavy weapons. We thought they were doing some exercises. My husband left me in front of the embassy and, as I walked through the entrance, the office boy came towards me. He was very distressed; "Memsahib," he said, very frightened, "The soldiers are around the town to kill, I am going home!" "Oh no!" I replied, "You stay here, keep the door closed and call me if anybody tries to enter." I went upstairs to ring my colleague. She had tried to ring me at home to warn me not to go to the office that morning, but I had already left.

After that the Ambassador rang me and told me to wait for him at the embassy. In the meantime I started to empty the filing cabinets into two large suitcases. In a short time the Ambassador arrived driving the embassy car himself. We carried the suitcases

81

to the car and sent the office-boy home. While we were loading the suitcases a small crowd of local civilians appeared and surrounded us. My fear was that they might think the two suitcases were full of money. It was a scary couple of minutes because they were ominously silent, not at all friendly, and their numbers were increasing rapidly. I got into the car and gave them a smile, somewhat forced in the circumstances, and said, *"Jambo!"* (Greetings) to them while the Ambassador got into the car. We drove forward through the crowd slowly and they parted reluctantly to let us pass. One or two of them began running alongside and thumping on the car roof but we soon left them behind. I heaved a large sigh of relief. We did not drive along the main street, Acacia Avenue, as we thought it could have been dangerous so we went through the back streets.

Suddenly, several bursts of gunfire broke out in the streets around us. The mutinous soldiers were using their machine guns to shoot down entire Asian families in their own homes. The shooting and crying was horrific. I will never forget it. There was nothing we could do to help the unfortunate victims. We could only witness the terror going on around us as we drove to safety. As soon as we arrived at the ambassador's residence I rang all the other embassies. Bad news all around! The British High Commissioner, the Canadian High Commissioner and the German Ambassador were all beaten up and robbed! At that time President Nyerere of Tanzania was a guest of the Sultan of Zanzibar on his yacht along the coast.

We kept the embassy closed for the following couple of weeks but, every morning, I had to go to check the offices and send a report to Rome, to the Ministry of Foreign Affairs, La Farnesina, about the latest happenings.

Every time I went to town I had to pass road-blocks manned by soldiers involved in the mutiny. They always asked me where I was going in the embassy car. *"Mimi na ku-enda ku-ona mama yango"* (to see my mother), was my reply.

82

Early one morning when I was still at home, some heavier gunfire started from the direction of the coast. Soon, all the mutinous army was assembled alongside the beach, lying behind the bushes with their rifles. British warships had just arrived from Mombasa to stop the revolt of the Tanzanian Army. From the warships, helicopters started to bring ashore a whole brigade with land-rovers loaded with heavy weapons. Jet aircraft were screaming overhead and several lorries with loudspeakers were touring the streets to urge the rebels to give in. After a short time the soldiers realised they could not withstand the power of the British Navy and they left the beaches and the centre of town to barricade themselves in the army barracks outside the city. The siege lasted ten days. On the last day all the mutineers surrendered.

Even then, the trouble was not over. Two political factions were still very much at war and every day we had some disturbances and gunfire. This went on for weeks until President Nyerere succeeded in restoring normal life again with the help of the British forces.

One day at the Embassy we had a visit from the manager of Alitalia Airlines, Carlo Morelli, who sadly passed away a few years ago. He came for some files regarding Italian citizens in Dar-es-Salaam. I had known him in Nairobi. He was very dedicated to his job and he loved '*Mamma Alitalia*', as he used to call the airline. He knew I had worked for East African Airways in Kampala. So, before he left the office, he smiled at me and said it would be more appropriate for me to work for an Italian airline as I was Italian and he offered me a job with Alitalia if I ever returned to Nairobi.

Because of my husband's contract with Agip Motels, one year later, in 1966, we went back to Nairobi. I was obliged to leave every job I had, like it or not, each time my husband moved! I started yet another new job in the booking office of Alitalia Airlines in Kenyatta Avenue, Nairobi. We had a small flat on the fourth floor of Kenwood House, not far from the offices.

I was very happy in my job. I was working with a lovely girl, Susan Thomas. She used to send all the Italian passengers to me with the words; *"Gemma, Italiano!"* We became very good friends and we are still good friends to this day. Luckily, I already had quite a good training in airline work so I did not find it difficult.

Living in Nairobi was very pleasant, with a good social life and many friends. At the end of one year my manager Carlo Morelli had arranged a free ticket for me to fly to London to attend the ballet *Copelia* at Covent Garden, something I had always longed to do.

Another Italian friend of mine, Rosetta Cooper, who was married to a British flower growing farmer, had a son, Romano, living in London. He met me with his girlfriend at the airport. They took me to the Cromwell Hotel first and later to the Covent Garden Theatre. After the ballet we had dinner in a Russian restaurant. It was a lovely evening. I enjoyed that trip immensely but, alas, it was over too soon. I went back in Nairobi but, once again, I was not there for long!

It was 1968. After less than two years my husband had the urge for a change again! This time it was to the coast North of Mombasa. One day he told me he had just accepted an offer to the manage the Whispering Palms Hotel at Kikambala. It was really a shock for me. Here we go again, I thought! Sadly and reluctantly I resigned my job with Alitalia. We wanted to keep the flat in Kenwood House but I still started packing everything I did not want to leave behind.

We arrived at Mombasa where we met the hotel owner and then we went on our way to Kikambala, twenty miles up the coast. When we arrived, the place looked empty. We could not find anybody. We walked over the lawn to the entrance and into the hall. In the end we found the previous manager and his wife, both drunk, sitting on the floor behind the counter of the bar! What a reception! What a start! It was certainly not a promising or pleasant

84

one. The hotel was in a very neglected state. It seemed to be our fate to get a place which always needed to be refurbished.

The hotel was located beside a lovely beach with fully equipped cottages in a complex of one-hundred rooms and suites with bath and showers. A swimming pool with an aquarium of rare tropical fish, two bars, tennis court, mini-golf course, table tennis and billiards room. It was a beautiful place but very hard work was awaiting us. This time I was in charge of the reception. We had only a staff of two African girls who could hardly speak English. Later, we recruited a very good receptionist, Liselotte, to help me with all the package tours for English, German and Italian guests. Liselotte spoke English and German and she was a big help to me. Very soon, we started building a new wing of another fifty rooms. Every Saturday and Sunday we had an evening of entertainment around the swimming pool with performances by a colourful local dancing troupe, *The Giriama*, and their band.

One evening we had a real treat! The famous American singer and jazz king, Louis Armstrong, who was staying at the hotel on a vacation, agreed to give a special concert in the hotel for the guests and an invited audience. Guests of honour were the Kenyan President Jomo Kenyatta and his wife, Mama Ngina. They were staying at the President's state house near the beach on the Mombasa road, not very far from the Whispering Palms. The President often used to come with his escort and bodyguard to have dinner, or a drink beside the swimming pool. We usually got just a half-hour advance notice of his visits. The concert was a big success. It started with his well known hit song, *What a Wonderful World*. Guests came from all along the coast and everybody had a great time. Security was always very strict when the President was at the hotel and it was even tighter on that occasion.

The work routine in the hotel was very tiring. Twice a week we had to cope with four Sharnow Reise package tours arriving from Frankfurt at four o'clock in the morning. I was in reception to welcome the guests and see they were served with refreshments and biscuits until their rooms became vacant at noon. Tourists were arriving at all sorts of odd times, especially in the high season, and I was often busy dealing with late arrivals. Sharnow Reise was a very good German travel agency and they always expressed their appreciation of the hotel management for our courtesy and care of their clients. We never had a single complaint.

Every year Sharnow Reise used to offer the hotel manager a complimentary return ticket to Frankfurt. My husband was not interested in making the trip but he suggested that I should accept the offer because it would give me the opportunity to visit my mother who, at that time, was living with my brother in Vienna, not that far from Frankfurt.

As soon as the hotel owner got to know I was going to visit Vienna he asked if I would be willing to take a suitcase of clothes to Budapest for him. His brother, a doctor, lived there with his wife and teenage son. They were short of everything, especially clothes and dress material. Customs was very strict and all such private imports were not allowed. There were very severe penalties for smuggling, even for trivial offences but he said nothing about that aspect of the matter. "It's just next door to Vienna" he said! My husband felt we could not refuse as he was our employer and so I had to take the suitcase with me. Wendy, the hotel owner's wife, on the other hand, was a very nice and understanding lady. She came next day and apologised for the heavy suitcase and how very grateful they were for my undertaking this dangerous task.

So, there I was on the flight to Frankfurt with only one heavy suitcase, on the top, just few of my own clothes with the remainder consisting of the 'contraband' consignment of new clothing and rolls of textiles material for Budapest. I changed to the Austrian airline at Frankfurt and flew on to Vienna's Swechacht Airport. I was so pleased to see my mother again that I had almost forgotten what I had to accomplish next. When I explained to my mother what it was all about and that I had decided to go to Budapest alone, she was horrified.

"You are not going alone, that is for sure, Filippo and I will come with you." she said.

When I left Mombasa airport with the hotel owner's suitcase the word 'expenses' was not mentioned and so, the journey to Budapest was made at my own expense. One sunny morning we travelled on a package tour from Vienna to Budapest on one of the river-boats that operate on the Danube. We were supposed to arrive in Budapest at lunchtime but about half an hour after our departure something went wrong. The boat broke down in the middle of the river, just opposite the gate of what looked like a concentration camp. It was surrounded with huge rolls of barbed wire. There were a number of lookout posts with armed guards and it looked very sinister. My mother gave me a worried look.

"We will never go back to Vienna." she whispered to me.

We had to wait for another boat from Budapest and transferred to that for the rest of the journey. We eventually arrived at the dock in Budapest at five o'clock in the evening. At the Customs Office we first had to give up our passports. We did not get them back until we departed three days later. There were about forty passengers and we were locked in a small room for another hour. The atmosphere was quite grim! At last the door opened and we were shoved, one by one, into a huge customs' inspection room with the usual long counters all around. Every passenger had their luggage overturned. We tried to stay at the end of the queue. Myself and my mother had only one suitcase, very heavy, between us and my brother had an overnight bag. Two tall women in uniform were doing the search. My brother had his bag overturned too but when our turn came i hoisted the bag on to the counter trying to make it appear light. I gave the official a smile and, pointing at my mother, I said as cheerfully as I could, "We have only one suitcase between us." She looked at us. My mother looked pale, because of the fear she was feeling. But she also looked so sweet and innocent, with her lovely white hair and her little hat with a black veil.

"You can go." The woman official said and left the suitcase untouched! I picked up the suitcase again and we walked to the exit. We all heaved a long sigh when we had got clear of the customs area. We were then driven in a coach to the hotel. I had the doctor's telephone number, but we had been warned not to make calls from the hotel because all the rooms were bugged. So, after dinner, I rang the doctor from a public telephone-box near the hotel and we fixed an appointment for the next morning.

We met the doctor and his wife in the hotel lounge. They handed me an empty suitcase. I left them having coffee with my mother and brother and I went to our room with their suitcase to make the switch-over. There was always a chamber-maid pretending to use the vacuum cleaner up and down in the corridor. I waited until she was at the far end and then I slipped quickly into our room, switched the clothes from one suitcase to the other and came out of the room as if it was the same light suitcase. The maid was still down the corridor. I went back to the lounge. The doctor had his car parked near the hotel entrance. We were all ready to leave but we had to pass with the suitcase in front of the reception where two guards in civilian clothes were permanently keeping a watch.

We shielded the doctor and the suitcase by walking in file at his side. We reached the hotel exit safely and the doctor placed the suitcase in his car boot. The whole episode made me feel as if I was involved in a major espionage operation! However, trivial as it may seem, there were plenty of stories of people being sent to prison in Hungary for even less serious offences than smuggling a few rolls of cloth. I thanked God when it was over!

The doctor and his wife turned out to be charming. Because we were leaving the next morning, they invited us to have dinner at the Cittadella, one of the best and most recently restored restaurants in Budapest, situated up the Hill of Buda overlooking the Danube. It was a wonderful evening, with a real Hungarian dinner. Back at the hotel they presented us with two beautiful pieces of Hungarian china, the famous 'Herend' and four records of Hungarian songs. I still keep the lovely china on display in my lounge as a souvenir of my 'operation cloth-roll'.

Next morning all three of the doctor's family were at the dock to say goodbye to us, like old friends. They are now in America. God bless them. I left Budapest with the feeling that one day I would return to that lovely city, and I did return, twelve years later to a newly liberated Budapest.

Back to Vienna, that fairytale city with which I had always been in love. I enjoyed the many beauty spots with the *Sound of Music* at every corner. The Hofburg, the Spanish Riding School with the Lipizzaner horses and Schonbrunn Castle with its magnificent gardens. That was the last visit to my mother while she was alive. The next time was to her graveside. She died in 1970.

At that time I had no need to support my mother any more. The villa in Italy was sold two years before and my brother bought a beautiful flat in Vienna. He had transferred all the collections of paintings and antique furniture to their new home. It was just right for their busy social life. One day, before I left Vienna for the last time, my mother looked around the and said to me, "Mouse, one day all this will be yours."

"I doubt it very much, Mutti," I replied quickly. She understood what I wanted to say, but she just whispered to me, "It is very difficult to live with your brother."

"Well Mutti, you wanted to be together." I replied. I knew then that she was unhappy. It was so sad for me to leave her. My fears proved right!

That was the last time I saw my mother. In 1970 I received a telegram from Filippo to tell me that mother was dead. The funeral had already taken place. A few days later I received a letter from

My mother with my brother in Salzburg shortly before she died.

The 'road' to Mogadishu.

him asking me to come to live in Vienna where he had arranged a job for me. I declined the invitation.

The new wing we had started to build at Whispering Palms at the end of 1968 was completed before Christmas 1969 and we had a very busy time dealing with many tours from Europe and America and from neighbouring African countries.

After Christmas we thought we would take two weeks holiday. I would have liked to go somewhere new and cooler, but no, my husband wanted to go back to Mogadishu to see old friends, and girlfriends! Over the years for better and for worse, I had always hoped he would change. What an delusion!

We decided to drive to Mogadishu. It was to be a long safari of around 960 miles there and back. Somalia had no roads, only tracks. The rainy season had not yet started but we just had time to drive back before all the roads would be closed in the middle of March. There was also the danger of being held up by the Somali Shifta, notorious brigands and smugglers, who regularly came into Kenya across the Somali border between Garissa and Beles Cogani. The Kenyan Police constantly patrolled the tracks but they could not be everywhere at once and the Shifta were skilful in avoiding them. On the journey from Isiolo to Garissa we were forced to drive very slowly because of the condition of the track. Suddenly, about ten Shiftas appeared out of the bush on the side of the road. They were carrying spears and some of them had rifles. They ran towards us shouting. Franco instantly accelerated and they chased us on the mud track for a some distance. I heard several shots from behind us but when I looked back I could see they were shooting wildly and throwing their spears as they ran after us. We could not drive fast because the road was full of potholes. Franco had to be very careful not to overturn the car or damage it. If we had been forced to stop, I have no doubt we would have been robbed and murdered. Thank God, Franco was a very good driver and we managed to lose them after a hectic time of fearful swerving and bumping up and down on and off the track. We finally left them far behind. About half an hour later it was dusk and we were lucky to come across a Kenyan Police Patrol camp on the track. We told the officer about the Shifta robbers and he took a squad of police back up the track in a land-rover. They returned about two hours later not having even seen a single Shifta. We spent the night safely there with them.

Mogadishu was no longer as we remembered it. The city was run-down and there were lots of people obviously unemployed. When Somalia was an Italian colony the people were generally poor but most of them had work of some sort. Now Mogadishu held an air of depression and the people seemed to me to be far less happy. I was glad when we left it.

The return journey was again not so peaceful for me. This time, for safety, we stopped before dusk at a Police Post near Liboi at the Kenya-Somali border rather than risk driving at night through the area where we had encountered the Shifta on the outward journey. We parked the car under a huge mango tree for the night and put up the tent. At dawn the next morning we rose and started to prepare for the long drive back to Mombasa. When we got in the car, Franco started the engine and I rolled down my window to take advantage of the cooler air from the headwind. I rested my arm on the open window and, just as we were about to drive off, out of the corner of my right eye I saw a black head with a little tongue darting in and out and the upper part of a black snake hovering near my head. I froze! The snake, it was a black mamba, was on the car roof. I was very frightened. I tried to whisper to Franco, "Stop the engine, there's a snake," but only a few of the words came out and they were in very high falsetto tones. Out of the corner of my other eye I saw Franco looking at me inquisitively. Then he too saw the snake. He switched off the car engine and whispered to me, "Don't move, I'll get out and you can come out on my side." He then opened his door and slid out of the car. I started to slide over on to the driver's seat while Franco came around to my side of the car. The snake started to follow me and put its head right through the car window. Franco was looking for something to hit it with but by then I had my head and shoulders out of the car and the mamba, a very poisonous species, fell off the roof and into the car. It bounced first on top of the passenger seat and then fell on to it. I pulled my legs clear just in time! I fell to the ground and scrambled away. We called the policemen and told them what had happened. They came back with a panga, found the mamba, which by then had slid to the back of the car, and chopped it into several pieces. Thank God, again! Apparently, the snake had been sleeping in the mango tree and had dropped on to the car roof when the noise of the engine had woken it up.

This also the year of the big break. On our return to Mombasa the late Toby Block, owner of the Brackenhurst and other hotels, offered my husband the job of manager of the Outspan Hotel and the famous Treetops in Nyeri. Our lives were at a crossroads by then. When Franco accepted the offer I had to make a heartbreaking decision. I had not been happy with our relationship for many years, mainly because of his philandering and so I told him, "We must separate."

He simply said, "I am sorry, I should never have married!" A pity he told me that only after nearly twenty years of marriage! There was not much left to make it worthwhile continuing to live together. Nevertheless, it was a friendly separation, then. He had to complete his commitment with Whispering Palms for another month. I decided to go back to Nairobi to live in the Kenwood House flat for which we had continued to pay rent. At least I had somewhere to go. He drove me to Mombasa and, before the train left the station he said to me, "Remember, from now on you are on your own!" I did not realise then that he meant for me to be alone still married to him, but not on my own to find happiness with somebody else.

In uniform with East African Airways.

Outside Lord Baden Powell's cottage at Treetops in Kenya.

CHAPTER IX

I was welcomed back to Nairobi by all my friends. They all helped me to face and resolve my difficult situation, especially in finding a job that I needed so much. The first to offer me a job was my good friend, Odilla, another Italian, who knew of my passion for fashion and beautiful clothes She owned a well known boutique, *Trés Joli,* in the Nairobi district of Westland. .

She asked me to help her run the shop, especially during the sales. I accepted happily. She used to go to Italy twice every year, coming back with all the latest fashions to the delight of the ladies of Nairobi. One day I had a telephone call from the Italian embassy. My friend, Bianca, the chancellor's secretary, asked me if I would be interested in taking a job as secretary to the commercial attaché who was shortly due to arrive in Nairobi.

Thanking her for the offer I promised to ring her back the next day. I wanted to talk to Odilla first. She told me she was sorry to lose me but I should not miss this opportunity and she said, with a smile, "I am sure you will be available if I need some extra help!" Whenever she called me afterwards I did return to help her. She deserved it. She was a very lovely lady and I will always remember her dearly. Sadly, she passed away last year.

Back to the Italian Embassy. I was the secretary of the commercial attaché. My husband and I were still on good terms and I used to spend the weekends at the Outspan and Treetops. In the hotel grounds of the Outspan the cottage where the founder of the Boy Scout Movement, Lord Baden Powell, was living before his death was still standing. It looked very neglected and on one of my weekend visits I asked my husband if I could have the key to the cottage. When I entered, an atmosphere of the past overcame me. His spectacles were still on his desk in the lounge along with some pencils and his fountain pen. In the desk drawers were many handwritten letters, reports and diaries. All the books were still in neat order on the bookshelves running around the walls and there were some framed pictures on the walls. A few of his uniforms were still hanging in one of the closets and, on a stand, his well-known hat.

When I returned the key, I asked my husband if I could restore the cottage into a sort of small shrine or museum. He agreed and said, "It will be another attraction for the hotel."

So, on my next week-end visit, I started to organise the cottage room by room. When the work was finished we had an official opening and a Boy Scouts Gala. Lord Baden Powell is buried in the Nyeri Cemetery where, every year on the anniversary of his death, a Scouts Gala takes place.

After one of my week-end visits on a Sunday afternoon, I was looking for a lift back to Nairobi so that I would be in the office on Monday morning. I met Vicky and Ken Grant who gave me a lift. We have remained very good friends to this day.

One day I organised a group safari for some guests of the Italian embassy together with some guests of the British High Commission. We went to Treetops with one night at the Outspan Hotel in Nyeri. At the entrance to Treetops you can see a lovely painting of Queen Elizabeth II who became queen in February 1952 when she was in Kenya at Treetops the day King George VI, her father, died.

There was an abundance of wild-life to be seen that night at Treetops. Herds of elephant (in Swahili, tembo), leopard (chui) and rhino (kifaru), were gathering to drink on the esplanade under the searchlights. Some buffaloes (mbogo) were fighting and Colobus monkeys (mbega) were cavorting through the branches. Suddenly one male elephant started chasing a female with a baby elephant. At the end of the chase, the male pushed the baby behind a bush and started to get amorous with the female. All the guests, who were watching from the terrace, were very amused.

The next morning we all fed the colobus monkeys with nuts and toast. Later, we all went on the road to Nanyki to stay at the Mount Kenya Safari Club. Our host, the famous Hollywood film star William Holden, gave us a splendid welcome in one of the most magnificent compounds at the foot of Mount Kenya. What a land of paradise it was at that time, our beloved Kenya. I will always treasure happy memories of that lovely country.

1970 turned out to be a year of destiny for me! That was the year I found the happiness for which I had been craving all my life. I have always been superstitious. Therefore, every year I used to visit an astrologer. I realised by that time that my life in Kenya had no further purpose and, in spite of my having many good friends there, because of my separation I was feeling alone in a small community. Even my best friend, Olga, did not know of my intention to leave Kenya. She used to come every Friday afternoon to Nairobi to take me to stay at with her at Tigoni Farm, in Limuru, to spend the week-end.

At the beginning of May, two weeks before my birthday, I went to see my astrologer, Sadruddin. That day I told him bluntly, "Mr Sadruddin, I want to leave Kenya!" I told him the reason why. He just gave me an astonished look and, in silence, started to lay down the cards with the 'Twelve Houses' in front of me. Then he smiled, saying, "You had better stay, because I can see that your luck will be in Kenya!" At that moment I had the feeling that it was the truth.

Months went by and one day, at a party, I met Noris, a lovely Italian lady, who was going to change my life. She was also separated from an Italian husband and was waiting for a divorce. This similar circumstance drew us together and we became good friends. We remain so today. We started to go out together and, because she had a car, she often picked me up to go to the cinema, shopping and to parties.

One day she came to my office. I remember it was the

beginning of November. "Gemma, would you like to come to my party on the eleventh?" she asked me. "There will be a friend of Howard's with us, he is a widower." Howard had been seeing Noris on a regular basis and was soon to become her husband.

November 11th. That evening I met Reggie! It was as if we had known each other already. He told me he was very lonely. His wife died the year before. Then he asked me if I was married. My answer was "I'm not married any more, I am not single, I am not divorced, I am in limbo!" He smiled, "I will not marry again." he said. Smiling too, I replied. "Me too, I had enough once!" Then we laughed together.

Now I wanted to ask him the date of his birthday to establish his birth-sign. "The twentieth-first of April." was his reply. "Oh! You are Taurus, same as me!" I replied. Smiling, he took out of his pocket a silver money clip with a Taurus engraved on the front and with *Destino* engraved on the back. "Do you like it?" he asked me." It's lovely," I said. He gave it to me. "It's yours, maybe it will bring you luck!"

At that moment I remembered Sadruddin's forecast. After the party he offered to take me home. It was not very far, less than ten minutes drive from Valley Road to Kimathi Street. That evening I did not know that the lovely house with the flat on the ground floor would be my future home.

That evening we had talked about each other's lives and of our friends, our habits, our interests, and our jobs. He was the sales manager for Kodak in East Africa. He was sharing the flat with a friend at the time. We parted with a 'good-night' handshake.

It was some weeks before I got a telephone call at my office. I assumed Noris must have given him my phone number. "Reggie Ford here, do you remember me Gemma? I wanted to invite you with Noris and Howard for dinner next Saturday, but they have already planned to fly to Bombay at the week-end. It would be nice if you could still join me."

100

It was the first of many dinners I was to share with Reggie. Noris rang me later. She was sorry that she and Howard could not accept the invitation but, "maybe it was for the best," she said with a laugh!

We started meeting regularly at the Muthaiga Golf Club. Reggie was a very keen golfer with a good handicap and he played nearly every day after office hours. He was also often away on safari. I started to join him on the golf course but only when he was not involved in a competition.

Reggie had served in the RAF during World War II. He was a photographer, flying reconnaissance missions over enemy territory to obtain intelligence pictures. During one mission his aircraft had been shot down off the coast of France. He was the only survivor of the crash and he had endured in a rubber dinghy for three days in the Bay of Biscay in the middle of winter. With no water and no food he had almost perished but, lucky for him, and for me, he was spotted by a warship just in time to save his life! After his recovery back in England, he took part in the Normandy D-Day invasion as a photographer, landing with the first wave of troops on 'Gold Beach'. Later, in the Arromanches area, he was wounded on a reconnaissance mission behind enemy lines. He was unable to get back but the French Resistance hid him in a cellar to avoid his being taken prisoner by the Germans.

Reggie's mother was an American from Boston. Reggie had gone to live and work in America in the 1930s but when the war started, he left America to enlist as a volunteer with the RAF. He was proud of that. After the war, his knowledge of photography secured him a good job with Kodak.

I did not know the details of Reggie's war service until years later, but I knew at the time that he was a brave and honourable man. I also realised I was in love, for the first time in my life. Better late than never! I had been very fond of Max, my cousin in Berlin who had died in Russia in the war, but that was more of a 'puppy

101

romance' that had never really developed. Who knows, if Max had lived? I had never really loved Franco, in the classical sense. I had married him because he was nice, at the time, and I felt an affection for him, but that had worn off over a period of years when I discovered the extent of his philandering and I simply felt stuck with him for years after that. Now, something had changed in my life. I decided to stop my visits to the Outspan. It was not right, I told myself. This was the first step to a complete freedom of mind and of heart. For me, it was a completely new sensation! I knew I wanted to see Reggie again. One evening at dinner, after nearly three months of going out together, Reggie put a ring inside my napkin. It was his way of proposing. He wanted to go to the Outspan to speak to my husband to ask him to give me a divorce.

I told him it would be better if I spoke to Franco. I thought of going to the Outspan the following week-end but news in Kenya travelled amazingly fast. Two days later I went home from the office during lunchtime and found him waiting for me in the flat at Kenwood House. There was no need for much conversation apart from me asking him for a divorce.

"Who is that man in the picture on your dressing-table?" He asked me as soon as I entered.

"He is the man who wants to marry me!" I replied.

"How can he marry you if you are already married?"

"I am not married any more." I told him.

"You will never get a divorce!" he said, and with those words he left. So much for his telling me I was on my own when we parted at Mombasa railway station!

It was 1971. Another year of change in my life and another struggle, this time to get a divorce! In the meantime I had to leave the flat now that my relationship with Reggie was coming into the open. Noris rang me one day, "I know you and Reggie are looking for a house. The flat on the ground floor here in Valley Road has been to let for weeks."

1943. RAF photograph of Reggie with his camera.

The house in Valley Road.

1972. Myself and Reggie celebrate Noris and Howard's wedding, and our own engagement.

Our wedding in Nairobi. 1973.

She gave me the name and address of the landlord. It was just what we were hoping to find. The flat needed to be redecorated and furnished. It was a lovely house with a beautiful garden, less than a mile from the centre of town. I wanted the flat to be ready for Reggie's birthday on April 21st. I was planning to give a housewarming party. Could we also say it was an engagement party?

Thanks to all our many English and Italian friends, the party was a great success. For me and Reggie it was a day of true happiness. All my colleagues from the Italian Embassy were there and among them dear Angelina, a lovely girl. I had known her since she was a teenager. She was the secretary to the Ambassador and she had all her life in front of her. Sadly she died in a tragic car accident. I will never forget her. Also my other dear friend Bona. She died peacefully in Nairobi in 1995. She was a distinguished artist, a wonderful painter. I still treasure three paintings she gave me as a wedding present.

We were so happy in Valley Road. In May 1972 Reggie had to go to Beirut in the Lebanon for a Kodak Marketing Conference. It was the first time we were apart, but I did not feel too lonely with the company of our dear friends Noris and Howard upstairs and Rin-tin-tin, a lovely ridgeback. Back from Beirut, Reggie brought me the best present I ever had, an unusual wedding ring in white gold. Also, Noris was planning her wedding with Howard for the coming December. Reggie and I were not so lucky. We had to wait until 1973!

Noris and Howard married on December 30th 1972. The threat by my ex-husband not to give me a divorce did not prevent me changing my name by deed-poll to Ford on May 22nd 1973 before we went to America. It was a first step towards my freedom and much longed for happiness.

1973 came as a year of luck and joy for us. In March, Reggie was selected as one of the team of senior golfers due to play for

Kenya in the World Senior Golf Championships in America at the Golf Club in Colorado Springs on August 2nd. It was to be my first visit to America and we planned to visit Kodak in Rochester, San Francisco and New Jersey at the same time.

Life was very pleasant in Valley Road. With many friends, we had a busy social life. Coffee parties, expeditions to the antique and curio shops with Vicky Grant, one of my best friends in Nairobi, and frequently entertaining visitors from Kodak U.S.A. Whenever Kodak visitors came to Nairobi, they used to say, "We are going to Gemma's for dinner!" One evening we had a Kodak 'People to People' party visiting Kenya. They were lovely people. The next day I organized a shopping spree in town for all the wives. I still have the little flags I used to put on the dinner-table to welcome the guests from various countries.

The General Manager of Kodak East Africa, Maurice Taffe, and his lovely wife, Margaret, were guests of honour. They were also good friends of ours and still are. Every Christmas we were invited to their beautiful villa at Nyali Beach on the Mombasa coast. One of those visits had a special happy memory when we met a lovely couple who also became friends, Nora (the Baroness) and Roy, who now live in Sussex not very far from us.

Muthaiga Golf Club was the meeting place of the Golfers' Society and the Kenyan team had a preparatory meeting there before leaving Nairobi on July 30th, destination Colorado Springs. Everything was well organised and, on arrival at the venue, each competitor was provided with a Pontiac car for the duration. The Broadmoor Golf Club in Colorado Springs was a magnificent golf course with a very impressive club-house building beside a lake and with luxury suites, four restaurants, a swimming-pool, a museum and even a zoo!

During the time Reggie was playing I was quite busy acting as interpreter for some of the teams who were not all acquainted with the English language, such as the Belgian, Italian and German teams. The committee was also organising outings for the ladies to the Colorado Mountains, (Cripple Creek), to pantomimes and fashion shows. The days were flying by, full of activities and on August 12th we had the award ceremony with Mr. Brinton Porter, the Chairman, presenting the prizes. A dinner and dance followed in the evening. On every table which had beautiful flower arrangements, and at each place, presented by the Belgian team, there were two golf balls, perfect imitations in white marzipan! It was an unforgettable evening! Kodak, from Rochester, sent each golfer a Kodak umbrella. The next day we were ready to fly to San Francisco.

I was immediately taken by that fabulous city; the cable cars, the mysterious China Town, Fisherman's Wharf and the fashionable shopping centre. We were staying at the Sheraton and every day we went to discover the beauty of the Californian coast: Monterey and Karmel in the South, the Napa Valley in the North with its famous vineyards. We enjoyed a wine-tasting at the friendly House of Sebastiani. We went further down the coast to Sonora on the Mexican border with the beautiful Geode. I will always remember, as we left San Francisco Reggie sang; "I left my wallet in San Francisco!" (With apologies to Tony Bennet).

From San Francisco, by invitation of Kodak, we flew to Rochester in New York State and a fantastic welcome. Nothing was too much trouble! Even an Italian singer was engaged to give me a welcome in the Hotel restaurant and a beautiful flower arrangement was placed in our suite. We were visiting the immense and very interesting Kodak factory. You have to travel in an electric car from one section or department to another so huge is the complex. All of the management and staff were really marvellous. There was a party every evening and one special party, on a hill, under a huge tent with a delicious barbecue served in the western style and with an impressive performance from a cavalcade of cowboys.

We left Rochester for the nearby Hackensack Golf Club. The manager, Arthur Lund and his wife, Eve, were good friends and we had a fabulous week there. Reggie in particular enjoyed this event as he was a very keen golfer with a good handicap. We were already at the end of August and it was time to go back to Nairobi to face the struggle for me to get a divorce.

Reggie was determined to get it settled before the end of the year. Because Reggie was to bear all the expenses, the lawsuit started on October 15th and on November 28th we got the *Decree Nisi*. What a relief to see the end of an untenable situation. On December 22nd 1973, on a glorious morning, we were married in the Attorney General's office. Witnesses were our best friends Olga and Carlo from Tigoni Farm. He was a famous lawyer and I could not have had a better adviser to help me to achieve a resolution to the case. He will be gratefully remembered always. Carlo died in Rome after they sold the Tigoni Farm and returned to Italy. Olga still lives in Rome and is still my best friend!

That morning after the ceremony we went back with Olga and Carlo together with all our friends to Valley Road. If I close my eyes, I can see everybody one by one, they are all there, happy for our happiness, united under two little flags, Italian and British in friendship together.

At three o'clock in the afternoon we were already on our way to Mombasa. That evening we were invited for dinner at the grill of the Nyali Beach Hotel by Margaret and Maurice Taffe, General Manager of Kodak East Africa. It was a delightful surprise. Lobster was served on a dish of ice! We had Christmas together in their lovely villa at Nyali with their son, Peter. "Happy Christmas". One Christmas to remember forever, and forever I will be grateful to my Italian friend Noris for helping me to find my happiness!

We went back to Nairobi for the start of the New Year in 1974 to resume our normal life. Happy ever after!

We went to a lovely party at the Muthaiga Golf Club that

The award ceremony in Colorado Springs. 1973

Maurice and Margaret Taffe with their son, Peter.

went on into the early hours and we had breakfast at sunrise! By late Spring we decided to have a short holiday in England where Reggie, two years before, had bought a flat in Brighton to be near his mother, Gertie and stepfather, Paul Compeyron, when he retired. When we arrived at the flat, I was enthralled by the beautiful view from the fourth floor out over the lovely Withdean Park. Just right for the two of us. A friend of Reggie's was staying in the flat, paying the expenses only, no rent, so we could take over the flat at any time. I loved it at once and I was already imagining our future life there.

Before flying back to Nairobi, we went for a week-end to Paris! One evening we were very late returning from the Lido and we could not find a taxi. I stopped an empty bus. The driver was charming! He took us to our hotel entrance. He did not want us to pay so Reggie gave him a packet of American cigarettes. That little incident helped to make our day! I was sorry when that little holiday ended.

After we had such a lovely holiday, a frightening time was awaiting us when we returned to Nairobi. Every Wednesday afternoon Reggie played golf with Gordon Duff at Muthaiga Golf Club. Odilla and I used to join them on the golf course. In the evening we usually had dinner together, alternating between their place and ours. They were lovely friends and we always enjoyed our evenings together. That first Wednesday evening after our return from holiday the dinner party lasted longer than usual and it was past midnight before Gordon and Odilla departed. We were both quite tired and went to sleep quickly. Something must have disturbed me because I woke up suddenly. Our bedroom door was always open and I noticed that the light was on in the passage. I thought Reggie was in the bathroom. I stretched out my arm, but Reggie was in bed, asleep beside me! I shook him awake. "Reggie, somebody is in the bathroom!" I whispered. He jumped out of bed and ran into the passage shouting, "God, it must be a burglar!"

113

It was. It was lucky they did not carry any guns at that time. Reggie called out to me; "Gemma, get my gun!" We did not have a gun but, just the week before, the Kodak Office had given us a siren, similar to those used by sailors on a ship. It was just the right occasion and I switched it on as soon as we realised there were burglars in the flat. It worked, making a terrific noise! That, along with Reggie shouting for a gun, made them run. One of the burglars was standing in the passage. When he saw Reggie, he ran through the lounge and out through the kitchen door carrying a bag of loot. They had drilled out the two locks of the kitchen door. I found the bits in the garden the next morning.

There were three of them and each one was carrying some loot when they made their escape. We called the police but by the time they arrived the burglars were well gone. All of our cutlery and the complete dinner service was gone along with many ornaments and a rare *bilau* (Arab dagger), a present from my dear friend Giuliana, We also lost a most beautiful zebra skin that had been hanging up in the entrance.

The next day one of my lady friends brought me some cutlery and plates. Luckily my friend, Anna Maggi, of Ceramic Industries, who made the dinner service for me, had kept the design so she was able to reproduce the complete dinner service with the same design in only three days. I still have the new cutlery set I bought that day!

The next day also, a policeman came to return the Zebra skin! With evident panic, the burglars had thrown the skin away in an empty plot near the Panafric Hotel where the police found it the following morning. I was already resigned to its loss forever. I was so happy to get the zebra skin back that I put it back in the same place in the entrance. Alas, it was not to be there for long! After less than two weeks the burglars came back one day when we were out. This time they broke-in through the front entrance! and the zebra skin disappeared for good.

114

After the second break-in, we decided, to deter them by welding all the window handles and putting bars on the windows. We had a month's respite.

Early one afternoon I was alone at home in the lounge on the phone to Olga. Reggie was still at the office. Suddenly I heard a crash in the bedroom. "Somebody broke a window," I said to Olga, "wait on the phone!" I ran to the bedroom. The side window near my dressing-table was broken and glass-splinters were everywhere but they could not open the window because the handle was welded. A trickle of blood was running down the remaining shards of glass. Obviously, one of the burglars had cut his hand badly. I saw two men dressed in dark suits standing on the small balcony on the ground floor. We used to call the balcony *Romeo and Giulietta*! As soon as they saw me they jumped off the balcony and ran away.

I went back to the phone where Olga was waiting, very concerned for me. I told her what had occurred and I immediately rang Reggie. He rang the police from his office and then he arrived home in twenty minutes. Later, the police arrived. "How many more times do we have to endure this?" I asked the policeman. He looked around; "Next time, when they come again, you wait behind the window with a kitchen knife. As soon as you see a hand breaking the glass, you cut his hand off!" Unbelievable! Sooner or later there was going to be a next time. How many more times would we have to undergo such an ordeal? The worry was becoming unbearable!. We then started thinking about returning to England.

It was always understood that Reggie would not retire from Kodak for another two years, when he was sixty-five. Our life in Nairobi was not as it used to be when we were free of all these nightmares! I began to believe that there was something supernatural behind it all and that I would always be plagued by something sinister and violent in my life, a Dark Avenger instead of a Guardian Angel! It was temporary feeling of paranoia but the course of my

115

life up to that time had seen me moving from one dangerous stage to another.

The reasons we seemed to be a target for persistent burglary attempts was a mystery to me for some time but then I began to think my ex-husband might have had something to do with these 'co-incidences'. He had been very angry when I divorced him and married Reggie. I knew well enough that he had often spent some of his spare time in the seedier parts of the cities in which we had lived. He knew lots of the local people who also frequented those places and I began to wonder if the Dark Avenger could be a jealous ex-husband. 'Hell hath no fury ...' does not necessarily only apply to a woman scorned! Why the burglars were so determined to rob us in particular and who might be responsible was something I could not be certain about but my mind was being affected and I knew I could not endure much more worry. I longed for peace.

This spate of burglaries precipitated a near break-down in me. I had seen too many wars and witnessed too many acts of violence. I had come close to death too many times and I began to think my luck would run out soon, just when I had found the happiness of a truly loving relationship for the first time in my life. I no longer felt safe in Kenya. We had reached a turning point and we had to decide to start a new life somewhere else. The consequences were to be so sad, to have to leave our lovely home, our many friends, for Reggie to leave the job that he loved, but it was a necessary decision. We fixed the date of our departure for June 15th 1975. We started to tell our friends. I also had start to undo what I had put together with so much love, our home!

Still, the most important thing was for us to be happy and to be together. We had something that nobody could take away from us. The Saturday evening before our departure Maurice and Margaret Taffe, on behalf of Kodak East Africa, gave us a lovely party at the International Casino. It was after one o'clock in the

116

morning when we returned to Valley Road. Reggie had developed the habit of going ahead of me to open the door to be first to enter the house. From the entrance I heard him saying; "Here we go again!" He was looking at the smashed glass of the, mercifully still unopened, window in the dining-room. Again, there was blood on the handle. If they had been able to open the window we would not have needed the Express Transport Company to ship our belongings! That was the burglars' last good-bye!

On our last morning in Nairobi we had coffee with all my lady friends. It was very moving! We exchanged presents and gave them all a warm invitation to our new Brighton home. That morning I was in something of a trance. I still did not fully appreciate the fact that we were leaving Kenya for good. It was if I was acting in a dream. It was not until I walked around to have one last look at the empty home and Valley Road that the reality sank in. In the garden, the agapanthus, the hydrangeas and the jacaranda were in full bloom. I have since heard from friends that the house and the garden are now in a state of complete abandon. There followed a final sad goodbye to our friends and to Kenya at the Embakasi Airport. "Kwaheri!" (Goodbye).

Happy together in our Brighton flat. August 1993.

CHAPTER X

After we had settled down in England, Reggie renewed his contact with friends, many of them veterans of World War II. In 1976, Reggie was again able to take up his beloved golf and he became a member of the Dyke Veterans of the Dyke Golf Club in Sussex. There, by the strangest coincidence, he met the very man who had helped him to get out of France and back to England during the war. What a small world!

The same year there was a beautiful warm summer and we started our European safaris! Our first was to Italy. But not everything was all right. The Avenger had another victory! Reggie's decision to leave Kodak and start his retirement two years early made a lot of difference to his financial affairs. It was not very long after we had settled in England that difficulties arose, due to the uncertainty of the monthly permit about money transfer to the U.K. More importantly, the value of the Kenyan Shilling dropping dramatically from 20 to 100 shillings to the pound. The worst aspect was that during the years of his retirement Reggie was never able to invest his money for a high return because of the uncertainty of the date of the payments. Sometimes it took up to three months for the payment to arrive and every month there was the same uncertainty.

This went on for years! Luckily, when Reggie still lived in Kenya, he paid for our state pensions in Britain and that, along with other savings we had, was a great help. It was also very helpful to have a good friend in Kenya, Maurice Taffe, at that time General Manager of Kodak in Kenya and for his assistance in sorting things out from time to time we were always very grateful.

Nevertheless we were determined to make our life happy and contented. We were together. we were both in good health and we were enjoying the company of our many good friends.

So, in July we were off to Genoa to stay with my god-daughter and her family. In spite of all the happiness I was now experiencing Italy was still a black spot on my life. It was always to be one for me because of my brother. Since my mother's death in 1970, we had lost touch completely. Reggie played golf in a tournament in Genoa and we spent one week there. Then we decided to go on to Vienna.

We planned our journey to Vienna through the Dolomites to Innsbruck. The landscape was enchanting. When we arrived in Vienna Reggie asked me, "Are you going to ring your brother?" He knew that I was not very keen to get in touch with him again. I looked in the phone directory. His name and the same address were still listed but I could not bring myself to ring him, a sort of fear was gripping me. All the harshness of the past years came back to me. Before we left Vienna I found my mother's grave. It was a sad and tearful discovery.

In 1978 I received the sad news of my brother's death from a severe stroke. The letter was from his housekeeper, Fraulein Poldi, still very energetic at eighty-six years old. She had been looking after my mother and my brother from the time they left Italy to live in Vienna. I learned from her letter that the flat, with all the contents, was already sold and that there was a bitter quarrel between the two solicitors representing the vendor and the buyer. She begged me to come to Vienna to collect a case of photographs and one of my mother's rings, the only one left. Fraulein Poldi wanted me to have it. So this was the end of the family's fortune!

On our arrival in Vienna, Fraulein Poldi gave me a full report of the last eight years from the time of my mother's death. We went to the grave together where this time mother and son were lying united in death. I was in tears but I said to Fraulein Poldi, "I cry for my Mutti but I can't cry for my brother!" She gave me a little smile, "I understand Frau Gemmina! She was an understanding lady. She died a few years later and I will always remember her.

I was not to go back to Vienna again until 1990, when we went with Vicky and Ken Grant to Budapest on a package tour. Then I had not enough time to visit my mother's grave again. Maybe one day!

In the meantime, back to England, we made a decision about our future life. Reggie and I were very much alike and in our married life we had very few arguments. So we agreed to take a nice holiday every year that would keep us fit and well. I know some people would not approve, thinking it is better to save the money. But we did not regret it. We had a happy time together and Reggie enjoyed every one of the last years of his life. Now I alone can rejoice in those memories. We live only once. Reggie was a very good driver; I was the navigator - a jolly good team!

In the winter of 1980 we went to Spain where our friends, Maquita and George Dixon had a flat in Benidorm. Through them we got a lovely flat on the Levante Beach. For me it was like being in Italy because of the similarity of the language and the type of food. We made many friends. One evening we had a real cosmopolitan party with guests from five countries; Spaniards, Italians, Germans, English and Scottish. At the end of the evening I had a headache after having to keep conversations going by translating from one language to another! Our friends from England, Dorothy and Cyril Hillman, came to stay with us and we had a great time together. Also visiting were our good friends from Kelso, Mary and Tom Abraham, who enjoyed their stay.

In August 1980 we again travelled from Dover to Calais, through France to Laon, Chamonix, Lake Garda and Venice and then down to Florence and back up to Genova. We had a lovely day together with Marina's parents, Teresa and Sergio. Marina was at that time, working at a bank in Ventimiglia. She had a lovely flat in a skyscraper looking down to the sea.

We persuaded Sergio and Teresa to join us on our return journey to Brighton, passing through Ventimiglia on the way to say

121

good-bye to Marina. We stayed at Auxerre on the way to Brighton and we had a great time together.

We went back to Italy in September 1980. This time to Florence and Rome and from there to the Dolomites to meet again with Marina, Teresa and Sergio. From there we went to Torino to see our Kenyan friends, Carla and Gigi Farinetti, in their beautiful estate, *Il Casale* in the hills outside Torino (Turin). For the next two years we made frequent trips to discover the beauty of the Italian Dolomites and the Austrian mountains and lakes.

In September 1982 we saw more lakes and mountains. This time in France and Switzerland. From Dover to Paris and on to Interlaken and Basel (Basle). There we met another very nice couple, Sheila and Philip Hardcastle, from Yorkshire. We have been good friends since then and visited each other many times thereafter. Reggie and Philip played golf together. We had a lovely time in Interlaken and enjoyed a sundowner drink on our adjoining balconies. In the meantime we went to Zurich to see our Kenyan friends, Mr and Mrs Lüdi. After visiting Lucerne, we went through Germany to Trier for a wine tasting in a famous wine cellar near the Porta Nigra, and then through Strasbourg back to Brighton.

In 1983 we went back to Genova for the wedding of Marina and Carlo. We had three wonderful days. Later, we went to Switzerland as guests of Antonio and Mimma de Santis with the lovely Alessandra. Doctor de Santis had been appointed as Consul of the Italian Consulate in Geneva. With them we had more wonderful days. But it was time to go back to England and we went back through Germany, Alsace and France.

Reggie always wanted to go back to Normandy. It was an emotional need. So, in May 1984 I was glad to organise a five day tour together with a very nice couple we had previously met in Benidorm on our first holiday there, Nita and Joe Pritlove. This time we went on the ferry from Newhaven on a lovely warm night and we arrived in Dieppe in the early morning. We took the coast road to Arromanches. This was where Reggie had landed many years before on Gold Beach.

He was the only walking survivor in his team when they had gone inland that day. All his comrades had been wounded by shrapnel. He went to knock at the first house he could find to get help. An old lady opened the door, looked at him and then shouted excitedly, *"Marie viens, les Anglais sont ici!* (Marie come, the English are here!) A young woman came to the door and she and Reggie looked at each other. Something clicked. Marie was a schoolmistress. Sometimes war promotes love as much as peace and they became more than friends. Marie's mother went to the garden to dig up a bottle of wine to celebrate the encounter.

After a few days Reggie joined another photographic team. This time their destination was a castle. It had been a German Headquarters and the Germans had left behind a lot of material, including quite a number of toys. Reggie took a cartload of toys to Marie's school, to the delight of all the children. They treated him like a hero!

Arromanches is a pretty little town. It was a lovely day in May and we decided to have a picnic. After shopping at the *Charcuterie*, we stopped near a small river at the back of a garden. Reggie suddenly realised it was near Marie's garden! "Would you like to see if she is still alive?" I asked him. "She must be an old woman now" We were all smiling "And I am an old man too!" Reggie replied, smiling broadly. We left it at that!

The visit to the war museum on the beach brought back many memories to Reggie. He was happy to have done his duty and to be still alive. Over the next two days we went to Caen and Honfleur. It was my birthday and we stopped at a lovely restaurant *La Forchette d' Or* (The Golden Fork). The French certainly know how to cook and eat. It was a fine meal.

Next we went to Mount San Michel with its mediaeval narrow streets. Back to England then but, before getting on the ferry in Dieppe we had quite a fright. Joe started to be unwell. Was it the Calvados he should. not have drunk? we wondered. He was diabetic and kept fainting despite taking his medication. The feeling that we might lose him was unbearable. Nita, his wife, was very worried so we quickly drove him to the emergency department of the nearest hospital and we stayed the night in Dieppe. The next day, thank God, he was much better and was able to board the ferry.

What a relief for us all. The sea was calm on the return journey and after four hours we arrived safely at Newhaven. Nita and Joe stayed with us until the next day in Brighton. Still, even with all the worry and excitement, the trip to Normandy had been very worthwhile.

Soon it was 1985. This time, with Vicky and Ken, we started our next journey from Dover to Ostend for a trip to Bavaria. We stopped one night in Bruges, a very picturesque town with lots of canals, a bit like a smaller Venice. We were bound for the Bavarian Castles, two of which, Herrenchiemsee and Linderhof, had some of their interior and exterior decorations made by my grandfather Giovanni. It was there we met a lovely couple, Hedeltraud and Adolf Mainhart from Hanover and we became good friends. We still are. It was a very nice holiday. So much so that we went to Austria again in 1986 to a beautiful spot on the river Danube, a little town named Weissenkirchen, which had endless vineyards and castles. From there to Mayerling to see the famous castle (now a convent) where Prince Rudolf, the son of Emperor Franz Joseph of Austria, committed suicide with Maria Vetsera. The place is steeped in history!

In 1987 we went back again to my beloved Genova! Marina and Carlo had been happily married for four years. The four of us had a wonderful holiday around the Ligurian coast of *Le Cinque Terre* (The Five Lands). We then went on to Santa Magherita and Portofino, where I had spent many summers as a little girl before going to the mountain resort with my grandmother.

For the following four years, our safaris had to stop! 1988 and 1989 were bad for us In January 1988, I broke my ankle on the golf course, on the 17th hole, not a lucky number for me! It took nearly three months for me to get back to normal, thanks to the help of a very good physiotherapist, Julie, at the Royal Sussex County Hospital. At the end of that year, in December, Reggie had to go into the Sussex Eye Hospital for a cataract operation on his left eye. Thankfully, all went well and he was back home after three days! During that time our good friends Vera and Eric Morgan looked after me at 'Abbots' their beautiful flat on the Brighton seafront, where Jody, their labrador, was a lovely companion for me.

In June of 1989, Reggie had a second cataract operation on his right eye, also very successful. After the second operation, on his last day in hospital, I will always remember the excitement in his voice as he looked out the window; "I can see properly again! all the colours, everything!" he said.

For two years after the operation there was no more talk about holidays! Then, in the summer of 1990 I said to Reggie: "If we don't go on holiday this year, we will never go again! I had a feeling, like a premonition, that it was to be our last holiday together.

I started to organize a coach tour to Vienna and Budapest with Vicky and Ken. At that time Hungary was starting to remove all restrictions on the tourist trade and we were one of the first tour coaches not requiring an entry visa. In the middle of August we left Dover for Ostend for a night stop-over at Brussels before starting the long journey to Vienna. Lovely weather, but it was very hot and crowded everywhere. Still, on the river Danube, we had some cooling breeze and the landscape was very picturesque.

We stopped near the Moelck Abbey and had lunch at Krems, a lovely little town. We arrived in Vienna in the evening. The next day we went around Vienna and got ourselves lost! The centre of city had changed because of the building of the underground railway. The day after that, we continued our journey to Budapest. Our hotel was about twenty miles outside the city in the middle of a lovely pine forest and we were able to sleep peacefully away from the usual city noises.

We had some nice excursions on that trip but the one to Lake Balaton was a little disappointing. I was sorry that Vicky could not get one of the terracotta vases she loved so much.

There was a very happy event in 1991! Gianluca was born. This lovely baby completed the happiness of his parents, Marina and Carlo, and of his grandparents, Teresa and Sergio. The first few years Gianluca was really a handful! Then he started to improve and became a very lovely well behaved boy. Now, he is the joy of his family and friends because of his alertness and intelligent approach to life.

During the course of the following few years we settled down to a quieter life. We had done enough travelling for our lifetimes. Reggie had left the Golf Club, but we still had our social life with a nice circle of friends.

For Her Majesty the Queen, and for me also, 1995 was an *annus horribilis*! Reggie's health was slowly deteriorating. It was to be the last year of his glorious life. We were still walking every day for almost two hours at a time but, after a while, he became more and more tired. He was eating less and less and did not sleep as well as he used to. The doctor could not find anything wrong but I still kept giving him all the same vitamins that I was taking myself. The big fright came at the end of March. One morning, coming back from our walk and not very far from our home, his legs collapsed and I had to quickly flag down a car in the London Road. The occupants were a very nice couple and they helped me to get Reggie back to the flat. I was very frightened and rang the surgery immediately we got home. It was 4pm. I told the doctor all the symptoms and that I had given him two paracetamols. He told me to give Reggie two paracetamols every four hours and to ring the surgery again if he was not better the following morning.

Next morning Reggie was much better, to my great relief. He did not want to go to the doctor because he thought it was just a chill due to the very cold wind, and he did not want to be a nuisance.

For nearly four months, Reggie was himself again, just taking things a bit more slowly. Nothing could have forewarned me of his sudden deterioration. That Sunday was a lovely summer day and we were sitting happily on the seafront. The next day, Monday 31st July at 6pm. Reggie started feeling pains. He was perspiring profusely. I rang the surgery and the doctor on call came within ten minutes. He told me Reggie needed an emergency operation. He immediately called the ambulance which arrived after twenty minutes.

The paramedics were very good. They kept him breathing as we sped to the hospital. I was sitting beside Reggie in the ambulance and he said to me: "It's very cold" They were his last words! On our arrival in the casualty department two nurses quickly took me away. Reggie died shortly after. There was no time left to operate. It was too late! A nurse came: "I am sorry, your husband is dead. He loved you very much; his last words were: "I don't want to die, I want to look after my wife, I love her very much." My heart stopped for a moment. "Oh no!" was all I could say. I cried then, as I cry now in the memory.

The diagnosis and cause of death was: Ruptured abdominal aortic aneurysm. He was eighty-three years old. That night I wished I was dead also! Reggie gave me his love, lots of happiness and a lovely home. It is already just one year since he left me, but I know he is still with me.

To-day, September 1st 1996, I end this account of my life. I have many people to thank for helping to make my life interesting and happy in spite of all the trials and tribulations. I am eternally grateful to them and I have listed them on the acknowledgements page. I have dedicated this account of my life to Reggie because he gave me love and happiness even though we were both middle aged when we met.

I had always regarded myself as a *Povera Ricca Bambina* because of the loss of my family's fortune in the war and because of the suffering I endured due to the circumstances of the war. I have been only seconds from death at the hands of a firing squad. I have lived through the hell of an unjust prison sentence. I have endured the unhappiness of a loveless marriage. I have lived in daily fear of murder at the hands of the Mau-Mau. I had a narrow escape from the Shifta cut-throats of Somalia, not to mention the encounter with the black mamba, and I have experienced the vindictiveness of the Dark Avenger. But out of all that had come true love, late but real.

It was worth waiting for. Thank you Reggie. You turned a poor little rich girl into a lucky girl, rich in something better than material wealth. Love!

CRISANTEMO BIANCO

Hai un' aria, triste d' abbandono,
o crisantemo bianco,
Quando tu offri stanco,
a tua corolla in dono.

E un dono, mesto, senza resa,
Un ultimo saluto,
A cio che s' e perduto.

Fra tante morte cose,
tu sei l' unico fiore,
L' emblema di un dolore
che un cuor fedele pose.

WHITE CHRYSANTHEMUM

You look sad, neglected,
O white chrysanthemum,
When you offer, tired, your blossom gift,
Without return, to what has been lost,
A last greeting.

Between so many dead things
You are the only flower,
The symbol of grief,
Placed by a faithful heart.

Gemma Ford
September 1st 1996.
Brighton.

129